REFLECTION OF THE AWAKENED

(MIRAT 'L-ARIFIN)

COMMENTARY OF SURAH FATIHA ATTRIBUTED TO
IMAM AL HUSSAIN (AS)

SADRUDDIN AL-QUNAWI

INTRODUCTION, TRANSLATION AND NOTES
SAYYID HASAN ASKARI

Zahra Publications

Zahra Publications

ISBN: 978-1-776490-17-2

First Published in 1983 by Zahra Publications

Distributed and Published by Zahra Publications
PO Box 50764
Wierda Park, 0149
Centurion
South Africa
Email info@shaykhfadhlallahaeri.com
www.shaykhfadhlallahaeri.com
www.zahrapublications.pub

Set in 12 point in Garamond

TRANSLITERATION

Arabic Letter	Transliteration	Short Vowels	
ء	ʾ	◌َ	a
ب	b	◌ُ	u
ت	t	◌ِ	i
ث	th		
ج	j	**Long Vowels**	
ح	ḥ		
خ	kh	اَ	ā
د	d	وُ	ū
ذ	dh	يِ	ī
ر	r		
ز	z	**Diphthongs**	
س	s		
ش	sh	وَّ	aw
ص	ṣ	يَّ	ay
ض	ḍ	يِّ	iyy
ط	ṭ	وُّ	uww
ظ	ẓ		
ع	ʿ		
غ	gh		
ف	f		
ق	q		
ك	k		
ل	l		
م	m		
ن	n		
ه	h		
و	w		
ى	y		
ة	t		

ACKNOWLEDGEMENTS

First of all I would like to recall a total stranger who after having heard me speak during the Ali Day Celebrations in Birmingham in 1979 almost forced me to visit his house which I did, and there after giving me food put into my hands a collection of papers which included the text of Mirat'l-Arifin. His name was Shahjahan. May God guide him unto His Way.

I should also place on record my gratitude to Abu Yusuf Muhammad Afzaluddin Nizami of Hyderabad from whom I learnt a great deal about certain aspects of the present text.

Finally, I offer my thanks to Shaykh Fadhlalla Haeri whose personality has a spiritual presence and whose word has effect both on the thought and the practice of all those who come into contact with him. May God bless him and his work.

I thank Zahra Publications for having agreed to publish Reflection of the Awakened.

Sayyid Hasan Askari

TABLE OF CONTENTS

INTRODUCTION

According to Brockelmann (S.I. 807), Mirat'l-Arifin is one of the works of Sadruddin al-Qunawi (d. 1274). In the Introduction to Sadruddin's 'Ijaz'l-Bayan fl Tawil Umm'l-Qur'an (Dayarut'l M'arif, Hyderabad 1949), Mirat-Arifin fi Multamis Zain'l-Abidin, is enlisted under the works of Al-Qunawi following obviously Brockelmann. But neither Mu'ajam'l-Mu'allifin (Vol. 9, p. 43) nor Zirkali's Min'l-A'lam (Vol. 6, p. 253) mentions Mirat'l-Arifin as Al-Qunawi's work. Miftah's-S'ada (Vol. 2, pp. 451, 452) also does not include it under Al-Qunawi's works. Kashfs-Zunun (Vol. 2, p. 460) mentions Mirat'l-Arifin with a longer title (Mira'l Arifin wa Mazhar'l-Kamilin fi multamis Zain'l-Abidin) without giving its author. We cannot therefore take Brockelmann's word as final. It seems that Brockelmann enlisted it under Qunawi's works without fully examining all the relevant evidence.

The problem of the authorship of Mirat'l-Arifin becomes highly complicated as it is also attributed to Imam Husayn, and it is this claim which we shall try to examine here in detail.

As far as the manuscripts are concerned, we have seen six manuscripts whose details are as follows:
1. Early Eleventh Century complete text (State Archives, Hyderabad: Tas 723 Arabic, 1012/1603);
2. Early Twelfth Century complete text (Salar Jung Oriental Manuscripts Library, Hyderabad: Tas 42 Arabic, 1131/1718);
3. (Middle Twelfth Century incomplete text (Salar Jung, Hyderabad: Tas 59/3 Arabic);

4. Late Twelfth Century complete text (Salar Jung, Hyderabad: Tas 232 Majmu'a 7, 1187/1773);

5. Early Thirteenth Century copy of a Late Twelfth Century Persian Summary and Commentary (Salar Jung, Hyderabad: Tas 168 Persian, 1171/1757); and

6. Early Fourteenth Century Urdu Translation (Salar Jung, Hyderabad: Tas 159 Urdu, 1305/1887).

Manuscript (1) is catalogued without any note on its authorship. So are Manuscripts (3) and (4). As far as Manuscript (2) is concerned, the correction is made in favour of Sadruddin Qunawi obviously following Brockelmann. The twelfth century Persian commentator (Manuscript 5) whose name is not given on the text makes it plain that it was the work of Imam Husayn. Towards the last part of his commentary he says:

"On the request of certain "Elders who are People of Certitude (صاحب يقين) I did the interpretation of the Arabic treatise of Mirat'l-Arifin. However, the 'speech' of the Imam is brighter than the sun. How could one dare to interpret it?" Similarly, the author of the early fourteenth century Urdu translation who gives the title of Mishkat'l-Mawwahidin for his text mentions Imam Husayn as the author of the treatise. He says:

This treatise, Mirat'l-Arifin, which was written at the request of Imam Zain'l-Abidin, is brought to a close. Its author is the Imam Hammiim Amir'l-Muminin Husayn Shahid, son of Asad'allah Hazrat 'Ali." The author of this manuscript (Manuscript 6) reports an extraordinary dialogue between 'Ali ibn Abi Talib and Kumayl ibn Ziyad without giving its source. We reproduce it here in English for the benefit of those who do not have access to the manuscript:

Kumayl ibn Ziyad, son of Ziyad Najafi, was one of the special companions of Ali ibn Abi Talib (Peace be upon him). Once it so happened that Kumayl asked: "Master, what is Reality (*haqiqah*)?" Ali ibn Abi Talib looked at him and said, "What business dost Thou have with Reality?" But Kumayl persisted and said, "Do I not have your confidence?" Ali said, "Yes, thou dost have all my confidence but only that which will overflow from me will fall upon you, and thou wilt know it in its proper state." But Kumayl further persisted and said: "Would people like you disappoint a seeker?" Then Ali said, "Reality is the unveiling of the lights of Majesty without pointing to them." Kumayl said, "Please make it clear." Ali said, "It is forgetting of the uncertain in the light of what is certain." Kumayl said, "Please make it more clear." Then Ali said, "Mysteries are unveiled on account of their overwhelming nature." Kumayl continued, "Please make it more clear." Ali said, "Unity is absorbed in Unicity." Kumayl said, "Make it more clear." Ali said, "A Light shines from the Dawn of Creation, and it glows through all manifestations of Unity." Kumayl said, "Please make it more clear." Then Ali said: "Put out the lamp, for already there is daylight."

This at least is clear: that from the twelfth century onwards both in Persian and Urdu circles Mirat'l-Arifin was seriously considered as a work of Imam Husayn. This also is clear that Brockelmann included Mirat'l-Arifin among the work of Sadruddin Qunawi without actually looking into the controversy regarding its authorship. The only way open to us is to compare Mirat'l-Arifin whose central theme is the Fatiha of the Qur'an with Sadruddin Qunawi's well-known work on the same theme already mentioned here, namely, Tawil fi Umm'l-Qur'an. Apart from the general features of the Fatiha which are discussed by every commentator and the references to its contents shared by Mirat'l Arifin and Qunawi's work on Umm'l-Qur'an and other works on Fatiha, there is a noticeable difference between Mirat'l-Arifin and Qunawi's work under consideration. Where the latter is a detailed and exten-

sive work, Mirat'l-Arifin is brief and compact. Some of
the major emphasis of the latter are absent in the former.
The approach is similar. The references to the mysteries
of the Fatiha are shared. The clear equation between the
Fatiha and insan'l Kamil as expressed in Mirat'l-Arifin is
not that clear in Qunawi's work. The way in which the
well-known tradition of Self-Knowledge as God-Knowl-
edge is explained in the Mirat'l-Arifin is not the same with
Qunawi. Moreover, the over-all style of Umm'l-Qur'an is
laden with philosophical and mystical expressions whereas
Mirat'l-Arifin is more direct and transparent. The comparison however does not prove beyond doubt that the au-
thors of these two texts are not different. Qunawi's book
on Umm'l-Qur'an ends with the following words:

تم الكتاب و الله يقول الحق و يهدى من يشاء إلى صراط مستقيم
و الأمر كله لله هو الأول و الآخر و الظاهر و الباطن

Mirat'l-Arifin is brought to its end by a different form of
Invocation. This involves another kind of objection.

It is said that the way in which Mirat'l-Arifin ends is not
that of an Imam. It is not a form with which the Shi'ites
are familiar. As a matter of fact, the manuscripts we have
seen do not have the same form of Invocation towards the
end of the text. Let us compare them:
In the Text used for the Present Study:

فاكتفينا على ما رحمنا و الله يقول الحق و هو يهدى السبيل و هو حسبنا
و نعم الوكيل اللهم صل على سيدنا محمد أول كل شىء و أوسط كل شىء و
آخر كل شىء كما تحبّ و ترضى و على آله و أحفاده و أصحابه و عشيرته
من الأنبياء و المرسلين و الأولياء الصالحين برحمتك يا أرحم الراحمين

Different Endings: Manuscript (1) 1012H

فاكتفينا على ما رحمنا و وفقنا على ما مضينا و الله يقول الحق و هو يهدى
السبيل و هو حسبنا و نعم الوكيل و صلِ الله على سيدنا محمد و على آله و
سلم تسليما كثيراً كثيراً
يا أرحم الراحمين

Manuscript (2) 113 lH

و الله يقول الحق و يهدى السبيل و هو حسبنا و نعم الوكيل و صلِ الله على سيدنا محمد و على آله الطيبين الطاهرين و سلم تسليماً كثيراً

It appears that the treatise comes to a close with

و الله يقول الحق و يهدى السبيل و هو حسبنا و نعم الوكيل

and the Invocations of blessings upon the Prophet, his Family and Companions are later additions for they vary from one manuscript to another. It is probable that these endings reflect the *madhhab* of the copyist, and not of the author. Beyond this the objection regarding the ending of the treatise is not worth pursuing.

The Arabic text from which the English translation is done is taken from a printed copy of Lahore which does not mention the date. Most probably it was printed between 1900 and 1920. The reason for selecting this text in preference to any of the texts of the manuscripts we have seen is that the latter are defective with certain omissions. For instance, in Manuscript (1) the following key passage is missing:

الله الذى خلقكم من نفس واحدة و هى العقل و جعل منها زوجها و هى النفس

In Manuscript (2) we read the following passage

إن الفاتحة تنقسم على ثلاثة أقسام قسم متعلق بالخلق و قسم جامع بينهما

instead of the complete details relevant here in the text used for this edition which is as follows:

إن الفاتحة تنقسم على ثلاثة أقسام قسم متعلق بالحق و قسم متعلق بالخلق و قسم جامع بينهما

As we are referring to the text, let us here introduce two other questions regarding it; namely, of terminology and style. As far as terminology is concerned, the main objection is that certain terms used in the treatise seem to have entered the Arabic language only after the Greek philosophical texts were translated, and hence, the presence of these terms provides a serious basis to doubt its authenticity as a work of Imam Husayn. We have discussed this objection in detail under the Notes wherever such terms require an explanation. At this stage we would like to point out this much that none of the objections in this regard can be a conclusive proof that the work is of later date. All the terms of Mirat'l-Arifin could have existed prior to the period of the translators of the Greek works and the emergence of the philosophical writings in the Arabic language. Furthermore, as we have made it clear under the Notes, each term may belong to a multiple discourse, and it seems that the translators and the philosophers appear to have considerably limited the scope of the terms. The central question, as far as Mirat'l-Arifin is concerned, lies in another very important and so far greatly neglected area, namely, how certain terms were used by the 'People of the House' *(ahl'l-bayt)*. We shall discuss this in due course.

The question of style is equally important. The objection here is that certain parts of Mirat'l-Arifin are in a style called *'saja'* which, as the opinion goes, emerged late and reached almost epidemic proportions by the fifth century of the Hijra. We shall soon demonstrate whether this objection has any validity and whether it can bring into serious doubt the authenticity of the treatise in question.

'Saja' is a particular mode of rhetoric in which at short intervals such words occur as rhyme though not being bound by a particular metre. *'Saja'* is of two kinds: (1) السجع المطرف, In this type the two words agree in the letter but not in the measure (for example:الأمم، الدم). (2) السجع المتوازى, in this type the two words agree both in the letter and in the measure (for example: القسم، القلم). The majority of the instances in the text is of the

latter kind. Most of them belong to the opening section of the treatise. This is the usual practice among the Muslims to start a *'khutba'* (oration) or a book with such words as are both appropriate and invocative of a sense of mystery, grandeur and transcendence, and it could all be aptly expressed through words that rhyme and are bound by metre. Mirat'l-Arifin is one of the best instances of this practice. Abdul Qahir al-Jurjani (Asrar'l Balagha) says that *'saja'* is both an expression and a form of meaning. A good *'saja'* is one which spontaneously appears out of the world of associations wherein the truly intended meaning resides. The meaning determines the *'saja'*, for the former is not only the communication of a concept or an image but also of an atmosphere which is a part of the meaning itself. As such, *'saja'* is not artificial but rather necessary to the life of the meaning with which it is bound. The bad *'saja'* is however one which is indifferent to meaning and rests wholly on the sounds of the words thus bringing both sickness and corruption to language. If we apply Jurjani's criteria, the instances of *'saja'* in the text under review fall under the category of *'ahsan'* (good). First of all, they are not only required by the fact that they constitute the opening of the treatise but also no other word except what is used to rhyme the foregoing word could express the meaning more eloquently. Secondly, there is no artificiality about them: each *'saja'* is a natural embodiment of a plane of awareness whose central question is to apprehend both the manifest and the hidden symmetries of existence.

Regarding the objection that *'saja'* was not a feature of Arabic prose during the first century of Islam, we would like to point out that it was one of those opinions held with least regard for facts. First, *'saja'* was present from the beginning of the Islamic times though it degenerated into a disease by the fifth century. Both the Prophet and the Imams used *'saja'* in its best form. Jurjani cites examples from the 'Hadith'. *'Saja'* is found in the speeches, prayers and sayings of Ali ibn Abi Talib and also in the devotional prayers of Ali ibn al-Husayn. Therefore, it is not right to doubt the authenticity of any text belonging to the early period of Islam just on the basis that it contains the *'saja'*. The fact however remains that the *'saja'* of Mirat'l-Arifin is one of its best examples and is born out of the vitality and richness of meanings and perspectives. However, this is not the place to examine in detail the mysteries concerning the origin of this form of expres- sion, its association with the spiritual levels of consciousness, and the symbolic values of the choice of a letter to repeat in the *'saja'*.

Let us return to the question of the authorship of Mirat'l-Arifin for, as we shall soon see, it has another dimension.

In the opinion of some people Mirat'l-Arifin could be one of the works of Abdul Qadir Jilani (d. 1166). Many things to which the Shi'ites object might appear to fit very well in the framework of this theory. For instance, the reference to Abu Huraira by Abdul Qadir Jilani suggests no problem whatsoever. The citation of the poetry of Ali ibn Abi Talib whom the writer of the treatise refers as "my father" *(abi)* is not difficult to explain, for Abdul Qadir Jilani could easily refer to Ali ibn Abi Talib as "my father" as he was one of his descendents, and in the Arab usage it is not unusual to refer to one's ancestor *(jad)* as "father". So there seems to be a very satisfactory basis to regard Mirat'l-Arifin as a work of Abdul Qadir Jilani. But there is a real problem: how to explain the reference to Zain'l-Abidin, for we do not know that any of the sons of Abdul Qadir Jilani was known by this title. Furthermore, the concepts and the terminology of Mirat'l-Arifin do not figure in the writings of Adbul Qadir Jilani. And again 'Talimat-i Ghouthya', as we shall refer to it later in detail, reproduces almost all the terms and formulations of Mirat'l-Arifin under "Teachings of Ali ibn Abi Talib for Imam Hasan and Imam Husayn". It is clear that the author of 'Talimat-i Ghouthya' did not regard Mirat'l-Arifin as a work of Abdul Qadir Jilani but consciously reproduced the teachings of Mirat'l-Arifin as coming from the source of *'m'arifa'* (gnosis), namely, Ali ibn Abi Talib. Shah Gui Gasan Qalander Qadri who wrote both 'Tadhkira-i Ghouthya' and 'Talimat-i Ghouthya' refers to the same verses of Ali ibn Abi Talib as they are found in the Mirat'l Arifin. Shah Gui Hasan may not have seen the full text of Mirat'l Arifin because he does not refer to this title. But this is not certain as we have seen Mirat'l-Arifin being given other names as well - Mazhar'l-Kamilin or Mishkat'l-Muwwahidin. It is quite probable that Shah Gui Hasan might have read Mirat'l-Arifin under some other title. But this is not the issue. More significant however is the fact that the body of teachings as presented in Mirat'l-Arifin was identified with the wisdom of Ali ibn Abi Talib, Imam Hasan and Imam Husayn. Not only the Qadriyyas but also the Chishtiyyas and Nizamiyyas considered Mirat'l-Arifin as the work of one of the *'Ahl'l-Bayt'*. This is demonstrated by Abu Yusuf Mohammad Afzaluddin Nizami of Hyderabad who recently published an Urdu translation of Mirat'l-Arifin mentioning Imam Husayn as its author. Afzaliddin is one of the 'Khalifas' of the famous Chishtiyya-Nizamiyya Sufi, Khaha Ahmad Nizami of Delhi. The fact that the copyist of Manuscript (2) gives his name as Murad Beg Nakhshbandi further proves that Mirat'l-Arifin was known in all Sufi circles including the Nakhshbandiyya. Before we give our theory on the authorship of this treatise, let us briefly refer to another question - the connection between Mirat'l-Arifin and lbn Arabi's thought.

There is a close parallel between some of the formulations of Mirat'l-Arifin and those of lbn Arabi (d. 1240). There is a general correspondence around the ideas of existence *(wujud)* and 'non existence' *('adam)*, essences *(ayan)* and worlds *(akwan)*, occultation *(butun)* and manifestation *(zuhur)*, beauty *(Jamal)* and majesty *(Jalal)* which are summed up in perfection *(kamal)*; human being *(insan)* and 'comprehensive middle' *(barzakh-i jamay)*; and the similarity of emphasis on the mystery of primal 'darkness' *('ama)*. One of the striking examples of resemblance at one point in the very beginning of the text is worth mentioning: we come across two extraordinary expressions: (1) "the most holy and ancient emanation *(fayd'l-aqdas'l-aqdam)*" and (2) "the holy and ancient emanation *(fayd'l-muqaddas'l-muqaddam)*." Now from a superficial point of view, the rhyming of *"aqdas"* (most holy) and *"muqaddas"* (holy) appears to provide the *"saja"* (a mode of rhetoric in which words appearing at short intervals rhyme). But when we look into lbn Arabi's 'Fusus'l-Hikam', we notice that the difference of *"aqdas"* and *"muqaddas"* is not a matter of mere *'saja'* but a profound distinction between the self-manifestation of the Absolute within Itself which is "the most holy and ancient emanation" which lbn Arabi also calls as *"zuhur awwal"* (the First Manifestation) or *"tajalli ghyab"* (Manifestation in the Invisible), and "the holy and ancient emanation" *(al-muqaddas'l muqaddam)* which represents the actualization of the archetypes in the concrete forms which lbn Arabi calls as *"zuhur thani"* (the Second Manifestation) or *"tajalli shahadah"* (Manifestation in the Visible). The Mirat'l-Arifin associates "ayan" (essences) with the atribute of *"aqdas"* (most holy) and they are the first manifestation in the invisible, whereas the atribute of *"muqaddas"* (holy) is mentioned in connection with *"akwan"* (worlds), and they are the second manifestation in the visible. The correspondence between Mirat'l-Arifin and Fusus'l-Hikam, as far as these concepts are concerned, seems to be complete, and this is not an ordinary correspondence. Should we then say that Mirat'l-Arifin being so close to Ibn Arabi's system is either his work or a work of his school (and here to recall

Sadruddin Qunawi is inevitable), or may it not be equally true that Fusus'l-Hikam is located within the School which Mirat'l-Arifin represents, namely, the School of the People of the House of the Prophet, a matter which we shall soon take up. However, there are several ideas in Mirat'l-Arifin which are absent in Fusus.

It appears that the heirs of the 'School of the People of the House' *(maktab-i ahl'l-bayt)* were many, and its teachings, both oral and written, came down into both Shi'iit and Sufi streams of thought. Mirat'l-Arifin provides an excellent example of this phenomenon. Whether actually written by Imam Husayn or not, we need to inquire into all the aspects of the question whether it really belongs to the School of the People of the House of the Prophet.

By the People of the House we mean the *'ahl'l-bayt'* (the Root House, the *bayt'l-asal*) of *'walaya'* - the House of Fatima, Ali, Hasan and Husayn, from Ali ibn 'l-Husayn to the Hidden Imam. By the 'School of the People of the House' we mean those persons who were associated with one or another Imam as disciples and also those who at other times were shown the Way directly or indirectly, and also the teachings that came out of the discourses, speeches, prayers and sayings of the Imams. The heirs *(warithun)* of this School were many: the Athna'ashri Shi'ites, the Ismailis, the Mutazalites, the Ikhwan'l-Safa, and the Sufis. Hence, the School from the beginning had diverse and conflicting advocates and supporters. We are not interested here in their conflicts nor with the validity of their claims as against others. What occupies us here is the paramount fact that the teachings of the People of the House flowed into many different streams and channels, and it is quite probable that a certain work or teaching of the Imam came into one particular stream, and others remained ignorant of it. We are at the threshold of a new era of Islamic studies: it is getting clearer now that much earlier to the development of mystical and philosophical thought of the ninth/tenth centuries there was another 'school' associated with the circles of the People of the House wherein great and far-reaching ideas were being discussed, shared and explored. Annemarie Schimmel (The Mystical Dimensions of Islam, p. 52) observes: "The discoveries about the earliest Sufis show that some of the definitions attributed to mystics of the ninth century can probably be dated much earlier. They also show how Shi'ite and Sufi ideas were, at that early stage, interdependent. But many problems await solution. The thoughts of J'afer (as-Sadiq) and, perhaps, other early mystical thinkers must have been at work beneath the surface, permeating the mystical life until they appeared in the sayings of a number of Sufis, all near contemporaries, who reveal the potential variety within the mystical life." And similar is the observation of Paul Nwyia (Exegese Coranique et language mystical) concerning Imam Ja'far as-Sadiq's commentary on the Qur'an that it reflects a profound insight into the mystical dimensions, and undoubtedly he was one of the greatest teachers of Sufism. However, extensive research into this little known field is required, and perhaps within a couple of years our understanding of the development of Islamic thought may be considerably revolutionized.

On the basis of the extent of our research at the present stage we can easily say this much that the School of the People of the House could have played an immense role in laying the foundations of many great ideas whose development and systemization we notice from the ninth century onwards.

The question of the chains of transmission of mystical knowledge, both oral and written, is one of the most exciting areas of study. No attempt has been made so far to at least offer some introductory study so that others who come after us could, through further research, establish what we now regard as one of the keys to the mystery of such an early flowering of spiritual knowledge in Islam.

The period of the Twelve Imams (632 - 874 - 940) is one of the most formative periods of Islamic thought. The number and the stature of the Sufis of this period and their influence on whatever emerged as the form of mystical life in later centuries (refer to Appendix) are matters for both careful and respectful investigation. If one goes through the Appendix where we have listed all the important 'ahl'l-Irfan' contempories of the Imams, one cannot but conclude that their teachings were received by various people and could have been preserved by them. As the groups settled down in terms of 'madhahib' (sects) and as relationships between them became more formalized, the great sharing which the period of the Imams symbolized was no more available. One group was not aware what treasures the other possessed. The greatest tragedy is however one when the group who possesses the treasure is not even aware of its existence.

To get a clear idea of how the teachings of the Imams were transmitted to various Sufi orders, we should see how the major Sufi Houses are linked with the Imams. It was their lamp from which all the other lamps were lit. Even a cursory glance at the links between the Imams and the Sufi Masters will let one know that the teachings of the Imams could easily flow into various channels, and this explains why Mirat'l-Arifin is known to many Chishtiyya and Qadriyya circles.

The outstanding work on one of the central themes of Mirat'l Arifin, namely, the Perfect Man, is Abdul Karim al-Jili's Insan'l Kamil. Al-Jili does not mention Mirat'l-Arifin, but all the important terms which characterize the Perfect Man in al-Jili's book are those of the Mirat'l-Arifin. We should again note that a teaching is transmitted in many ways. It is not necessary that the book which contains it should be available to everybody. The very history of the idea of *'insan'l-kamil'* is a testimony to this aspect of how a given teaching becomes fragmented and later reconstructed. But how could al-Jili arrive at almost the same terminology as that of the Mirat'l-Arifin? The obvious answer is that he took it from Ibn Arabi whose works he interpreted, and who was his spiritual guide and intellectual mentor. But who was Jili's master, Shaykh Sharf al-Din Isma'il al-Jabarti? Was he a Qadriyya Master? And it is also well-established that al-Jili was a descendant of the founder of the Qadriyya order, Shaykh Abdul Qadir Jilani. Most certainly, al-Jili was initiated into the Qadriyya teachings, and was well-grounded *(rasikh)* in their mysteries. Al-Jali should have been the recipient of some of the teachings of the 'People of the House' as any other Qadriyya Sufi.

Mirat'l-Arifin is a compact statement. It uses both concepts and symbols. The movement from the conceptual to the symbolic is sometimes so fast that it is difficult to identify the stage of awareness associated with one or the other. Not one but several readings of the text will make one familiar with the domains and the stations involved in the course of moving from one paragraph to another. It is a journey into the mysteries of the World, Man and God. The very first change in our consciousness is effected by a tremendous sense of unity which pervades the text. A non Muslim reader who is not familiar with the Qur'anic terms and symbols is likely to be put off, for the text uses the Qur'anic symbolism throughout. A Muslim reader is bound to be perplexed because the most familiar words seem to obtain strange and baffling aspects. Such is the shock of the shift from the literal to the symbolic. More important than all this is the slow discovery that the Qur'anic terms are not merely terms of the so-called Qur'anic Studies but signs of another language which can be learnt only though

initiation. Hence, when we refer to the symbolic, we do
not mean here the symbolic in opposition to the literal in
the ordinary sense, but to a language which is the mode of
communication between the prophets and saints of God.
We ordinarily know it as a reflection into the mirror of
our faith, and yet its true meaning is far above our grasp.
Hence, to argue with the text using our ordinary methods
of discourse will be a futile act. The thing required of us
is to learn from it to what level of consciousness the text
both in parts and as a whole is a reference.

My advice to a reader who is not familiar with the
Qur'anic terms is to approach the text as he starts to learn
any new language. He will be in a far better position than
a Muslim who takes his familiarity with the terms to be
the knowledge of the terms. Except for the terms there is
nothing in the text which will create obstacles for the first
reading of the text. The best way is to take a pen and put
down on a separate piece of paper all the equations which
the text is offering between the symbols. At the head of
each equation there is always the reference to Being and
Knowledge. The pivot of the entire message is the relationship between 'being' and 'knowing'.

The text itself contains the explicit reference to its
theme - *tahqiq fatiha'l-kitab* (inquiry into the Opening of the
Book). The inquiry starts with the reference to the well-
known formulation: what is in the entire Qur'an is in its
Opening. What is elaborated in the Qur'an is epitomized in
the Opening *(fatiha)*. The Opening is in fact a summation
(ijmal), and hence the point under the letter, *ba*, is the final
symbol of the epitome of all knowledge. To call the Opening of the Book the Source of the Book is to define the
latter after the principle of summation and totality. The
Mirat'l-Arifin revolutionizes the concept of *'kitab'* (book)
by saying that this world is in fact two-fold, the world of
command *(amr)* and the world of creation *(khalq)*, and each

is a book from the books of God; and for each is a fatiha. In other words, for each there is a *'umm'l-kitab'* and
a *'kitab'l-mubin'*. Real knowledge consists in knowing the
'umm'l-kitab' of each realm, but Human Being, as we are
told, is a comprehensive book among the books of God,
and a *'barzakh'* for both the Divine and the Cosmic Realities. Hence, to know both the worlds is to know Human
Being. Self-Knowledge is the knowledge of all things of all
places and all times, for Human Being is the summation of
all things. So, Human Being is the Point and the Pivot, the
Fatiha and the *Umm'l-Kitab*.

On the basis of the Prophetic Tradition which is very
well documented in the traditional collections (see the
Notes) concerning the three divisions in the *Fatiha* - one relating to *Haqq* (God), one involving both God and Human
Being, and another only Human Being, the Mirat'l-Arifin
deals with the most difficult of all the problems, namely,
how God and Human Being are related. Of course, one is
Haqq, and another, *'Abd*; but how are they related in terms
of Being and Knowledge (*dhat* and *ilm*). Human Being being a comprehensive book from the books of God should
then be a comprehensive middle *(barazakhjam'i)* between
God and the World. To say that Human Being is this kind
of *'barzakh'* is to say that what is in God with respect to
summation and totality is also in Human Being: "One who
knows himself knows God". But here are very grave dan-
gers, and precisely from this point that religions have gone
the way of *'batil'*. Hence, Mirat'l-Arifin clears all doubts
and refers to this mystery as follows:
"As it is, his (Human Being's) knowledge is His (God's)
knowledge and his being is His being, but without requiring integration *(ittehad)*, incarnation *(hulul)*, or becoming
(sairura). For it is impossible to speak of integration, incarnation, or becoming without presupposing two existents,
whereas here is only One Existence, all things being extant

therein but non-existent by themselves. Thus, how could any of these things be conceivable between God and Human Being who is extant in God but non-existent by himself?"

Abdul Karim al-Jili interprets this mystery in his own way (and the influence of the formulation as offered by the Mirat'l-Arifin is quite obvious):
"Perception of the essence consists in thy knowing that thou art He and that he is Thou, and that this is not identification, or incarnation, and that the slave is a slave and the Lord is Lord, and that the slave does not become a Lord nor the Lord becomes a slave. (Insan'l-kamil: i.29, 16).

While al-Jili takes care to reject 'identification' or 'incarnation' without giving the reason, Mirat'l-Arifin, as the citation here shows, gives the most irrefutable of the arguments - how could one presuppose two existents whereas here is only One Existence?

Mirat'l-Arifin seems to use Man *(insan)*, Perfect Man *(insan'l kamil)*, and Humanity *(insaniyya)* as interchangeable terms. It so appears that whoever has the *'ma'arifa'* (self-knowledge) is the Perfect Man. Or, in other words, whoever realizes that all humanity is one undivided self *(nafs'n-wahida)* is in the real sense Man. All men and women are potentially 'perfect men' depending on the levels of their self-knowledge. For such *'ma'arifa'* there is no division of the outward and inward, for as Ali ibn Abi Talib says:

$$\text{فلا حاجة لك من خارج}$$
$$\text{و فكرك فيك و ما تفكر}$$

Nothing is excluded from Man. Both, all humanity and all the worlds, visible and invisible, are in him. This view is generally the same as that of either Ikhwan al-Safa or of Ibn Miskawaih. They talk in terms of the macrocosm and microcosm. They see in Man all the components that are in the universe. lbn Miskawaih however takes care to point out that the elements which constitute the world are in Man but not in their simplicity but in a composite mode, for Man is composite. It appears that they are closer to the concept of model *(nuskha)* and not to the idea of a mirror *(mirat)* which is a symbol central to Mirat'l-Arifin, for the issue is not what constitutes the world and the man but what Man is with respect to Being and Knowledge.

Fariduddin Attar (d.1220) echoes the view of Mirat'l-Arifin:

بر دو عالم خودتوئى بكردت	تو لموز جان جمله عالم
برجد مع فوانى شود زوماصلت	لوح محفوظ است در معنى حدلت
خود ز خود أيات حق رابازياب	در مفنيت خودتوئى أم الكتاب
عارف أشياء كماسى فود توئى	صورت نقش إلى خودتوئى
من شناس علم اللآدم توئى	انتخاب نسخة عالم توئى
برجه بينى خدد توئى بكر بدان	تو بمعنى برترى از أنس وجاب
بردو عالم را نمايد در ريسك	از كمال قدرتش بين فى دشك
بردو عالم رادرد بينال كند	نفتش آدم را رقم نوع زند
مطلع الفجر مش يمين كنقتديم	ست اتمال برزخ نور و ظلم
جون نمايد توسلوم اوست	برزخ جامع خط بويدم اوست

We cannot go beyond this brief introduction to the conception of Man in the treatise under review. The history of the idea of the Perfect Man as it originated in the School of the People of the House until it was given an elaborate and systematic statement by al-Jili required a separate study altogether.

Mirat'l-Arifin provides the only available argument in a systematic form for the well-known saying of Ali ibn Abi Talib:

مَنْ عَرَفَ نَفْسَه عَرَفَ رَبَه

The knowledge of the self as a way to the knowledge of God is the basic principle of *'tasawwuf'*. We can say this much here that it is only in this saying ("One who knows his self knows his Lord") that we have the basis for the unity between the theistic and the monistic approaches. We do not know of any other similar formulation from within any other religious tradition which resolves the conflict between the monistic and theistic approaches in such a way as does the Mirat'l-Arifin.

It is only in this treatise that we are given certain principles to decode the mystery letters that appear in the beginning of some chapters of the Qur'an. We have listed all such letters in the Notes. But we should warn the reader not to start decoding these letters and speculating about their meanings without fully grasping the principle used with respect to the interpretation of "Alif Lam Mim", the letters with which the second chapter of the Qur'an begins. One should however go through the whole text of Mirat'l-Arifin and study it with the help of somebody who is sensitive to the symbolism of letters *(huruf)* and possesses insight into the hidden meanings of the Qur'an.

Mirat'l-Arifin is again unique in offering another principle. As we know by now, the concept of *'fatiha'* (opening) is central to its system. So also is the concept of *'barzakh'* (the middle which partakes of both sections of which it is a middle). We are shown how to work out this principle with respect to *'bismillah'* (the Invocation which heads every chapter of the Qur'an except the ninth chapter). We are told that for each *sura* (Qur'anic Chapter), verse, and word, there is a *'barzakh'* whose identification will reveal a knowledge which is still a secret. We advise our readers not to start identifying it unless they work under a God-fearing guide. We are here very close to a great secret.

We are grateful to God that a work of such importance was entrusted to us for presentation in the West, and that He helped us complete it. We ask for His forgiveness for referring to certain matters whose knowledge is only with Him. And we pray:

O God, send Thy blessings upon Imam Husayn and the People of his House and his Companions, and guide us in the Way of truth and sincerity.

We thank Abdul Rahman Salem who went through the Arabic text and suggested a few corrections regarding the phonetic signs. There were four word corrections:

(1)Read أَسْأَل instead of أَسْئَل.   (Page 5 Line 1)
(2)Read مُسَمَّاةً instead of مُسَمَّى.   (Page 26 Line 10)
(3)Read الْمُنَبِّه instead of الْمُنَبِّهَة.   (Page 28 Line 7)
(4)Read تَنْقَسِمُ إِلَى instead of تَنْقَسِمُ عَلَى.   (Page 30 Line 8)

We are grateful to Professor John Hick for reading the English text of the translation and suggesting a few improvements.

110 Winchester Gardens   Sayyid Hasan Askari
Northfield
Birmingham B31

April,1983

THE TEXT OF TRANSLATION

MIRAT'L-ARIFIN
(Reflection of the Awakened)

In the Name of God, the All-MAerciful and the Compassionate:

All praise is for God who took out of Nun[1] what He held within the Pen *(al-qalām)*[2], and brought into existence *(al-wujūd)*[3] out of His generosity what He had treasured[4] within 'non-existence' *(al-'adam)*[5], and ripped open what was sewed up and manifested what was concealed.

All praise is for God who taught by the Pen which was entitled 'the Source of the Book' *(ummu 'l-kitāb)*[6] and by the 'preserved Tablet' *(al-awhu 'l-mahfuz)*[7] which was 'the Detailed Book' *(al-kitābu 'l-mubin)*[8].

All praise is for God who elaborated and enlisted in the Soul *(al-nafs)*[9] what was epitomized and decreed in the Intellect *(al-'aql)*[10]; and drew out the 'tablet' *(al-lawh)*[11] with His right hand from His left side as He caused Eve to issue forth from the side of Adam[12]. Thus, in the words of the High and Holy God, "God is He who created you all from one undivided self *(as-nafsu 'l-wāhida)*[13], and that was Intellect; and He made from it its companion, and that was Soul; and brought out from both many a man and woman, and those were 'intellects' and 'souls' *(al-'uqul wa al-nufus)*.

All praise is for God who manifested from *'al-habba'* (literally, blowing mist)[14], known as *'al-hayūla'* ('matter')[15] and *'al-'anqa'* (a fabulous bird, a metaphor for matter in motion)[16], the form of the universe *(ūratu 'l-alam)*[17], and differentiated the heavens and the earth from *'al-ratq'* (literally, a patched garment) known as the supreme element *(al-unuru 'l-a z̄am)*[18].

Glory be to God who individualized the essences *(al-uyun)*[19] through His most holy and ancient emanation *(al-faydu 'l-aqdas wa'l-aqdam)* and formed the worlds *(al-akwan)*[20] through His holy and ancient emanation *(al-faydu'l-muqaddas wa'l muqaddam)*, and manifested the eternal through the temporal, and the temporal through the eternal.

Glory be to God who unrolled the Parchment *(al-riqqu'l manshūr)*[21] and inscribed the Book *(al-kitābu 'l-mastūr)*[22] wherein was unfolded through letters[23] and words[24] what was within the heart of the speaker[25] where He first formed and established them and afterwards wrote and arranged, organized and perfected them (in the form of a book).

In *al-Fātiha* (the Opening Chapter of the Qur'an) He inscribed and epitomized what He set forth in detail in *al-Kitāb* (the Qur'an); what is in *al-Fātiha* is in the *Bismi'llāh* (the Invocation with which the Opening Chapter begins: "In the Name of God, the Compassionate, the Merciful", and what is in the *Bismi'llāh* is in the *bā* (the second letter of the Arabic alphabet with which the first word of the Invocation begins, namely, b-s-m), and what is in this is put within the Point (*nuqta-* the sign under the letter *bā*); and thus He concealed and obscured everything that was in it.[26]

May God send His blessings upon the Greatest Name *(al-ismu 'l-a'zam)*[27], the Compassionate Teacher and Promoter of Spiritual Causes through the most clearly established word that is Muhammad in whose Name He opened the book and brought it to completion; and distinguished truth from untruth and light from darkness. Blessings be upon his family and companions, and salutation.

O my son, I agreed to fulfill your wish when you asked me to put down in writing what God ordained in me concerning the truth of *al-Fatiha*[28], which was 'the Source of the Book' as it was by this name that the people of God and His elect referred to it *(al-Fatiha).* I call this treatise *Mir'at'l- Arifin fi multamasi Zayni'Abidin* ('Reflection of the Awakened' written at the request of Zainu 'l-Abidin).[29]

I beg for help from the Creator of the universe, for He is the One who alone is sought for help, and on Him alone one should rely. Know, then, my son, well-supported as you are, that this world is two-fold: the world of command *(al-amr)*[30] and the world of creation *(al-khalq)*[31], and each is a book from the books of God, and for each one of them there is an 'Opening' *(al-fatiha).* And all the things (pertaining to the world in question) that are set forth in detail in the book are summed up in its *'fatiha'*. With respect to it being a summary of what is set forth in detail in the book, it is called 'the Source of the book'; and with respect to it being an expansion of what is summed up in its 'fātiha', it is called a Detailed Book *(kitābu 'l-mubin)*, and thus the status of each in respect to what each contains is adequately indicated by the name after which it is called.

Everything that exists is a letter *(harf)*[32] in one respect; a word *(kalima)*[33] in another, an isolated and separated entity in one respect[34]; and a compound of words in one respect;[35] and a *'sūra'* in another[36]. If we look into each existing thing without looking at its modes *(wujūh)*[37], properties *(khawās)*, accidents *(awārid)*[38], and concomitants *(law-āzim)*[39], abstracted as it were from the totality, it is with respect to this abstraction that we designate it as a "letter' *(harf)*; and if we look into its modes, properties, accidents and concomitants, and relate it to the totality, it is with respect to its being related to the totality (and the totality related to it) that we designate it as a 'word' *(kalima)*. And with respect to its abstraction from all that exists in terms of relations *(mansubāt)* and correlations *(madāfat)*[40] and in terms of distinctions between one and another (of this type), it is designated as belonging to the category of isolated and separated letters *(huruf muqāta'a mufrada)*; and in terms of distinctions between such and such and also of intermingling of such and such, it is called a 'compound of words'-and in respect of the distinction between the compound of words, and in view of everything existing on its own level, it is called a *'sura'*.

When you have understood this, know then that God *(al-Haqq)*[41] is the Origin and the End of all things; unto Him is the returning of all affairs, and to Him belongs their outcome.

It is beyond question that everything was in Him before it came into existence, and this also is beyond question that He is in everything. He was and there was nothing beside Him. He is as He was[42] So His Being *(dhāt)*[43] is 'the Source of the Book'*(ummu 'l-kitāb)* with respect to all things contained therein, and His knowledge is 'the Detailed Book' *(al-kitābu 'l-mubin)* with respect to the details set forth therein regarding what is contained in the Being that is 'the Source of the Book'. So, all things are contained in it: His knowledge is 'the Detailed Book' with respect to details, and 'the Source of the Book' with respect to their summary and generality, as the tree is contained in the seed. What we have referred to as 'the Detailed Book' is a mirror for the Being that is 'the Source of the Book', and knowledge[44] is manifested in the Being because knowledge is that by which Being is identified.

Thus, the Source of the Book' *(ummu 'l-kitāb)* which stands for Being *(al-dhāt)* and 'the Detailed Book' *(al-kitābu 'l-mubin)* which stands for knowledge *(al-ʿilm)* are from the Divine Realities[45]. The Pen *(al-qalam)* which refers to the Source of the Book' *(ummu 'l-kitāb)* and the Tablet *(al-lawh)* which refers to 'the Detailed Book' *(al-kitabu 'l-mubin)* are from the Cosmic Realities.[46] Thus between Being *(al-dhāt)* and the Pen *(al-qalam)* there is correspondence of both generality and totality, and similarly there is likeness between knowledge *(al-ʿilm)* and the tablet *(al-lawh)* in the details and with respect to the manifestation of things in them as particulars. Hence, the Pen *(al-qalam)* in its status as a Cosmic Reality is a mirror for Being *(al-dhat)*: what therefore is contained in Being in respect of generality and totality is present in the Pen *(al-qalam)*. The tablet *(lawh)* likewise, in its status as a Cosmic Reality, is a mirror for knowledge *(ʿilm)*. What is in knowledge with respect to the parts and particulars is manifest in the Tablet in the same way.

It has been pointed out that the world of command *(amr)* is a book from the books of God, and for it there is an epitomized book called *'umm 'l-kitab'*, and a detailed book, the *'kitab 'l mubin'*. The epitomized book is the Intellect *(ʿaql)*, and the detailed book is the Tablet. Likewise for the world of material dominion *(mulk)*[47] there is an epitomized book, and that is the Throne *(ʿarsh)*[48], and a detailed book which is the Seat *(kursi)*[49]. Thus with respect to what is contained in detail within the *'kursi'* being summed up in the *(ʿarsh)*, the latter is called *'umm 'l-kitab'*, and with respect to the details of the *'kursi'*, it is called *'kitab 'l-mubin'*.

Between the *('arsh)* and the *(qalam)* there is correspondence with respect to generality and totality (all things being in them), and likewise there is correlation between the
'kursi' and the *'lauh'* which can be viewed from three stand-
points: first, both belong to the level of manifestation;
second, both involve the division of one principle into
two principles; and third, both refer to the manifestation
of things in them with respect to particulars and details.
Therefore, the *('arsh)* for this reason possesses a tangible
status and as such is a mirror for the *(qalam)*: whatever is in
the *(qalam)* with respect to generality and totality is likewise
reflected in the *('arsh)*. The *'kursi'*, like the *('arsh)*, possesses
a tangible character and as such is a mirror for the *'lawh'*:
what is contained in the *'lawh'* is also confirmed in the
'kursi' with respect to particulars and details. The *'qalam'*
which is called (*'aql*) (Intellect) is a model of *'dhat'* (Being),
its mirror, its manifestation, its revelation and its radiance;
and the *'lawh'* which is called *'nafs'* (Self) is a model for the
'qalam', its mirror, its manifestation, its revelation, its radiance; and the *'kursi'* is a model of the *'lawh'*, its mirror, its
manifestation, its revelation, and its radiance. Thus (*'aql*)
(Intellect) is a transcript[50] of (*'aql*) (Being); the 'lawh' is a
transcript of (*'ilm*) (Knowledge); the *('arsh)* is a transcript
of the *'qalam'*; and the *'kursi'* of the *'lawh'*. But the Perfect
Man is a comprehensive transcript incorporating in him
all the transcripts.[51] He it is who is derived from the whole
(and he is the whole), and as such is comprehensive of
both the Divine and the Cosmic Realities.

The Being of God is a Book which envelops all, and
therefore is the origin of, and the link between, all books
before they are given a detailed existence; and His Knowledge is the Detailed Book which manifests in full detail
what is hidden in the *'dhat'* (Being). Likewise, the Perfect
Man is a book which includes all, and is the origin of, and

the link between, all books after they have been given a detailed existence; and his knowledge is a Detailed Book which manifests in detail what is in a summary form in him. Thus, the knowledge of the Perfect Man is a mirror for his being, and his being is manifest in his knowledge and individualized by it. Likewise, the Knowledge of God is a mirror for His Being, and His Being is manifest in His Knowledge and identified by it.[52]

Thus, between the Being of God and the being of the Perfect Man there is a correspondence with respect to generality and totality, as all things are in both for the same reason. And between the Knowledge of God and the knowledge of the Perfect Man there is correspondence in terms of the elaboration of what is in a summary form. Thus, the Perfect Man is a perfect mirror for the *'dhat'* (Being) of God because of this correspondence, and the *'dhat'* (Being) illumines it (the being of the Perfect Man) with respect to the totality and the summation of all things therein. Thus what is present in the *'dhat'* of God with respect to totality and summation is present in the Perfect Man in the same respect: and what is manifest in the knowledge of God with respect to details and particulars is also manifest, as in a mirror, in the knowledge of the Perfect Man in the same respect. As it is, his (Man's) knowledge is His (God's) knowledge and his being is His Being, but without requiring integration *(ittehad)*, incarnation *(hulul)*, or becoming *(sairura)*.[53] For it is impossible to speak of integration, incarnation, or becoming without presupposing two existents, whereas here is only One Existence, all things being extant therein but non-existent by themselves. Thus, how could any of these things be conceivable between God and Man who is extant in God but non-existent by himself?

If you hear about 'integration' (between God and the Perfect Man) from the People of God or find reference to it in their works, do not mistake it for what one could obtain between two existents. They mean by 'integration' no more than, and nothing besides, the Witness of One, Absolute, Real Existence *(shuhud 'ul wajud l-Haqq'il wahid 'lmutlaq)*;[54] and this means that the whole is extant with Him, and hence the whole is joined with Him in the sense that everything exists with Him and does not exist by itself - not in the sense that for the Absolute there is a separate existence with which the whole is joined, for this is untenable.

And for the Existence that is One *(wujud 'l Wahid)* there is manifestation *(zuhur)*,[55] and that is the world; and there is concealment *(butun)*,[56] and that is indicated in the Names; and between them there is a middle world *(burazkh)*[57] which partakes of both, and keeps them apart so that the manifest may be distinct from the hidden, and this middle world is the Perfect Man. Then, the manifest is a mirror for the manifest, and the hidden is a mirror for the hidden, but what is between them is a mirror that reflects collectively and in detail both the manifest and the hidden or an intermingling of both.

Having demonstrated this we now turn to what we were saying before; that as between the Being of God *(dhat 'l-Haqq)* and the being of Man, between the Knowledge of God and the knowledge of Man, there is correspondence; and as whatever is in one is in the other whether generally or in terms of the particulars, so between *'qalam'* (Pen) and the Spirit of Man,[58] between *'lawh'* (Tablet) and the heart of Man, between *('arsh)* (Throne) and the body of Man, and between *'kursi'* (Seat) and the soul of Man[59] there is correspondence: each one of them is a mirror for the other, for each is a likeness of the other. Hence everything that is in *'qalam'* in a condensed form is in the spirit of Man in a condensed form; what is in *'lawh'* in an expanded form is in the heart of Man in an expanded form; what is in *('arsh)* in a condensed form is in the body of man in a condensed form; what is in *'kursi'* in an expanded form is in the soul of Man in an expanded form; and thus Man is a comprehensive book containing both the Divine and Cosmic Books.[60]

We have considered earlier that, as with respect to God whose knowledge of His Being necessitates His knowledge of all things, and as He knows all things on account of the knowledge of His Being, so we may say with respect to the Perfect Man that his knowledge of his being necessitates his knowledge of all things and that he knows all things on account of the knowledge of his being; for he is the sum of all things, general and particular. Hence, whoever knows his self, knows his Lord; and knows all things.[61]

Therefore, my son, your looking into your own self is sufficient for you because there is nothing that is excluded from you. So this is what my father, Ali Ibn Abi Talib, the Prince of Believers, says in one of his poems:[62]

Thy sickness is from within thee - thou perceivest not;
Thy remedy is from within thee - thou seest not.
Thou thinkest thou art buta small body,
Whereas within thee is folded a vast world - thou
ponderest not.
Thou art that manifest book
By whose letters the hidden is revealed - thou readest not.
Hence, thou needest not anything from outside-
Thy thought (secret) is right within thee - thou
thinkest not.

(And it is in view of this that we are led to understand the words of God, to whom is all honour and glory): "Read from thy book: enough is thy self *'nafs'* on this Day to be a judge over thee,"[63] Thus whoever reads this book (of one's self) indeed comes to know whatever has happened, whatever is happening, and whatever will happen. If you are unable to read the entire book, read a part of it, whatever you are able to read. And also remember what God, the Sublime, says (in His Book): "Soon shall We show to them Our signs in the heavens and in their selves *(nufus)* so that it is made manifest to them that He is the Truth."[64] And also, "into your selves do you not see?"[65] Furthermore, "alif, lam, mim: That is the book wherein there is no fantasy."[66] *'Alif'* (Alpha) stands for unicity *(ahadiyya)*[67] of Being, that is Reality *(haqq)*, in view of which He is the First from the origin of all origins. *'Lam'* (L) signifies existence generously extended to *'ayan'* (essences). *'Lam'* is for existence a *'qiyama'* (support), and that is *'alif'* and for it there is a *'zail'* (hem), and that is the circle of *'nun'*, which connotes the circle of the cosmos. Thus, the joining of the *'qiyama'* with the *'zail'* (the circle of *'nun'*) is the mark (that is *'lam'*) of the extension of existence to the entire cosmos. And *'mim'* (M) refers to the Perfect Man who is a cosmos in himself. *(kaun'l-jama'y)*[68]. Thus, *'alif'*. *'lam'* and *'mim'* are a book wherein there is no fantasy. Hence. "Say: 'Enough is God as witness between me and you, and one who possesses the knowledge of the book.'"[69]

Thus, my son, He is the Book and the knowledge of the Book, and you too are a book. Your knowledge of yourself is the knowledge of the Book, and the Book contains everything: nothing wet or dry is left out of it.[70] One refers to the world of dominion *(mulk)* and another to the world of the celestial beings *(malakut)*,[71] and there is nothing higher than it except the manifest Book, which is you. The book that is sent down upon the Perfect Man[72] is a description of the grades of totality and generality and of the particulars and details regarding humanity. But the

Perfect Man himself is in the grade of unity *(wahdat)*[73] and universality *(jamiyyat)*. The Book, however, gives details of his (Man's) grades when it distinguishes between his stations and levels, between his states and cycles,[74] between his being, attributes and actions, for he (the Perfect Man) is familiar with the Being and the Names, with the Attributes and Actions, with the worlds and those who reside in them, with the grades of the worlds and those who possess them, with the conditions of the worlds and those who are associated with them; and he is familiar with every location[75] from all locations and with the demands of the inhabitants of each world both generally and in detail. These are the details of the grades of Man: he is the summation of all things.[76]

It must be clear now that the Qur'an is an introduction to Man and describes his grades both generally and in detail. And for this book sent down to the Perfect Man is a *'fatiha'* called *'umm 'l-kitāb'*. What is elaborated in the Book is summed up in the 'fatiha'; and what is in the *'fatha'* is in the *'bismillah'*; what is in the *'bismillah'* is in the *'ba'*; and what is in the *'ba'* is in the *'nuqta'* (point). Hence, the *'fatiha'* is the origin of the Book and the whole Book. And in the Book there are isolated and joined letters, words *(alfaz)*, 'Words' *(kalimat)*, Chapters *(suras)*, and Verses *(ayat)*. The Book is the sum of them, since there is nothing other than them. So whoever knows what we have said may know the meaning behind the words of God: "Do you not look at your Lord how He stretches the shadow? If He had wished, He could have made it stationary."[77] So the stretching of the shadow is the extension of the point of existence and its determination in accordance with the divine and the cosmic letters. "The stationary shadow" *(sukun)* signifies the absence of the extension of the point of existence and its determination according to the divine and the cosmic letters, and also the absence of remaining on its 'simple' plane, a matter which is clearly indicated by the Divine utterance: "I was a hidden treasure".[78]

Thus the point of *'ba'* signifies the point of existence, and the *'ba'* of the *'bismillah'* is a reference to the Second *'umm 'l-kitab'*[79] and that is the *'qalam'*, and there is no doubt that in it everything was enlisted. The *'bismillah'* is a reference to the Third *'ummul kitab'*, and that is *('arsh)*, and there is no doubt that the *('arsh)* was enlisted in the *"'aql"* (Intellect) which was *'qalam'*. And the *'fatiha'* is a reference to a comprehensive book, and that is Man *('fatiha'* = Man), and there is no doubt that *Man was present before his manifestation in all the grades of creation as all things are present in him after his manifestation.*[80]

The extension of the *'nuqta'*[81] (point) is a reference to the First Detailed Book *(kitab 'l-mubin)*; the extension of the *'ba'* to *'sin'*[82] refers to the Second Detailed Book; the details of the letters constituting the *'bismillah'* and the intermingling of one with the other therein refer to the Third Detailed Book; the repetition of the letters of the *'bismillah'* in the *'fatiha'* and the resemblance of some with other letters therein refer to the Fourth Detailed Book; and the entire Qur'an from *'fatiha'* onwards is a reference to the grades of creation and components thereof.

This being understood, know then that the *'fatiha'* has three parts - one part is related to God alone; another, to the world of creation; and another partakes of both. It is related from Abu Huraira:[83] "The Prophet said, 'Whoever performs prayer *(salat)* and does not recite *'fatiha'* which is the *'umm 'l-kitab'* is deficient (in his prayer)'; and the Prophet repeated this three times."[84] It means that whoever does not recite the *'fatiha'* in his prayer leaves it incomplete. Then Abu Huraira was asked: what about it when we pray behind the Imam. He said: Read it in your mind, for I once heard the Prophet say:[85]

> God has said, 'I divide the prayer *(salat)* between Myself and My servant, and for My servant what he asks of Me. When the servant says, 'Praise be to the Lord of the worlds', God says, 'My servant has praised Me.' When he says, 'God, the All-Merciful, the Compassionate', God says, 'My servant has glorified Me'. When he says, 'He is the Lord of the Day of Judgement', God says, 'My servant has honoured Me'. When he says, 'Thee alone we worship, and from Thee alone we seek help', God says, 'This is between Me and My servant, and for whatever he asks of Me.' When he says, 'Guide us unto the right path, the path of those Thou hast blest, not the path of those who have received Thy judgement, nor the path of those who have gone astray,' God says, 'This is for My servant to whom I grant whatever he asks of Me.'

Thus from the beginning of the Fatiha to the 'Lord of the Day of Judgement' is that part which belongs exclusively to God; 'Thee alone we worship, and from Thee alone we seek help' is related to both God and His servant; and from 'Guide us unto the right path' to the end of the Fatiha is related only to the servant. To demonstrate these three parts, draw a circle and divide it into two sections: one is for God *(Haqq)*; the line in the middle is for that part of the Fatiha that belongs both to God and His servant; and the other division is for the servant only. (See page 18 of the Arabic text).

Know then that this entire circle includes all existing things and all domains, whether divine, spiritual, or middle, and the kingdoms relating to these domains. That which is related to the servant is divided into two sections: spiritual *(malakut)* and material *(mulk)*, for man is both a spirit and a body. That which is related to spirit is called *'malakut'* and that which is related to body is called *'mulk'*. But that which is related to both God and His servant is the Total Human Reality *(haqiqat'l-kulliyyat'l insaniyya)*.[86]

As the domains that refered to the servant were divided into two sections - spirit and body, they could be further divided into two more sections: one, 'the People of Felicity and Guidance' (signified by "Guide us unto the right path, the path of those Thou hast blest"), and the other, 'the People of Burdens and Wilderness' (signified by "not of those on whom Thy judgement hast come down, nor of those who go astray"). This is so because the domain of the divinity *(jabarut)* encompasses both Majesty *(jalal)*[87] and Beauty *(jamal)*[88], and it is inevitable that each should be manifested so that the commands regarding them could be made explicit and distinct. Hence, 'the People of Felicity and Guidance' stand on the right hand and are the manifestation *(mazhar)* of divine beauty and grace. And 'the People of Burdens and Wilderness' stand on the left and are the manifestation of divine majesty and justice. It is inevitable that these two groups should have different stations *(maqamat)* wherein the commands that relate to them, the behaviour they represent, and the actions they commit, are made explicit and distinct; and these stations are heaven and hell. All these are included in that part of the Fatiha which is related to the servant *('abd)*.

But the domain that is related to both God and His servant is that of the Total Human Reality, and its grade is that of Perfection *(kamal)*.[89] The people of this grade are the People of Perfection, and their station is on high as of a light that can be seen by all. Their abode is that of the Noble Ones scattered in all directions to the ends of creation. They stand at *('araf)* as God says: "At the *'Araf'* are such men as recognize one another by their shining appearances."[90] They envelop all the worlds (and all worlds are in them); and for them is Perfection that belongs to Being *(dhat)*. Both Majesty and Beauty are enlisted in Perfection, and the People *(arbab)* of this station are those who truly know God and His Unity.

When this is clear, know then that it is in this *'barzakh'* (the middle world) that God puts on the attributes of His human servant - laughing and crying, joking and ridiculing, suffering and disease, hunger and thirst and many things similar to these; and the servant puts on the attributes of God - life and knowledge, will and power to do things, expansion and contraction, and dominion in the cosmos, and many other things. Thus, this *'barzakh'* is a stage of the descent of the Lord *(tanazz' l-rabbani)* wherein the Lord puts on the attributes of the servant, and at the same time a stage of the ascent of the servant wherein the servant puts on the attributes of the Lord; and this is the 'blindness' *(ama)* mentioned in the famous hadith.[91] But fearing I might prolong this discussion and deviate from our main concern with the Unity of God, I do not mention here the secrets *(asrar)* of the mystery of *'amayya'*. So I stop here and restrict myself to elaborating what is suitable for this brief essay on the truths of the Fatiha.

It must be clear now that the Fatiha of the Book is inclusive of all the grades and all the worlds. As all the grades and the worlds are reflected in it, it is for this reason that it is called the Source of the Book *(umm'l-kitab)*. But the *Bismillah* whose name also is *'umm'l-kitab'* is divisible into two parts: one related to Being *(dhat)*, and that is *'bsm'* (In the Name of...), and the other to its attributes, *Rahman* and *Rahim*. What is between them faces them and partakes of them, and both are gathered in it, and that is Allah. To demonstrate this, draw a circle (See page 41 of the Arabic text) and divide it into two equal sections: write *'bsm'* on the right, *Rahman* and *Rahim* on the left, and Allah in the centre. This is the Name pertaining to Being *(dhat)* involving all Names and Attributes, and that is *'barzakh'* for it incorporates both the divisions in the circle.

Know then that the *Bismillah* [92] includes three Names - Allah, *Rahman* and *Rahim*, and also includes *'barzakh'* that partakes of them. As for Allah, His attributes are of three kinds: potential, actual and real. The real are those which support the actual and the potential attributes. So draw another circle (see page 42 of the Arabic text): write 'the actual attributes' on the right, 'the potential attributes' on the left, and 'the real attributes' in the centre *(barzakh)*.

Rahman' is the Name of God with respect to the extension of existence to all existences, and *Rahim'* is His Name associated with His giving to some a special existence. God by nature is *Rahman'* (All-Merciful) for all, and is for this reason *'Ar-Rahman'* (the All-Merciful). But the gift of special existence is associated with His Name, *'Ar-Rahim'*. He wills the emergence of the recipients of His Mercy so that the mystery of His *Rahmaniyya* is manifested through them; and He wills the emergence of the actions, deserving of reward, so that the mystery of His *Rahimiyya* be revealed through them. Hence, the attribute of Mercy is shared between three affinites: *Rahman* (merciful to all), *Rahim* (compassionate to some), and *Marhum* (the Recipient of Compassion). So, understand this, and draw a circle (see page 44 of the Arabic text) for this Name: write in the division on the right *Ar-Rahman*, on the left, *'kulliyat'l-maratib'* (totality of grades), for *Rahma'* is extended to all things, and everything on the scale of this extension is *'marhum'* (recipient of compassion), and write in the middle *Rahma'*.

And draw likewise another circle for the Name *'Ar-Rahim'* except that instead of *'Rahma'* in the centre write *'Rahmat'l wujudiyya'* (Mercy of Special Existence) which is related to good works so that the people who are under this Name are men of faith who live their faith through good works; and write in the division (see page 66 of the Arabic text) on the right *'Ar-Rahim'*, and on the left, *'Mo'min'* (believer), and *'Rahma'* in the middle.

Thus, what is valid for the principles (set forth here) is equally valid for their derivations. So, for each letter from the letters of *Bismillah* and of Fatiha and for each *sura* (Qur'anic chapter) in general and for its ayat (Qur'anic Verses), *'kalimat'* (words) and *'huruf'* (letters) there is a circle divided into two sections with a *'barzakh'* (middle) partaking of both.

There is no room for further details. It is impossible to refer to all the mysteries of Divine Wisdom. "Say, if all the oceans are used as ink to write down the Words of Thy Lord, they will soon be empty before the Words of Thy Lord be recorded, and this will be so even if they bring other oceans like them."[93] God says the truth. He alone is enough for Guidance on the Way, and He is the best of all supporters. O God, send Thy Blessings upon our Master, Muhammad, who is the first of all things, the middle of all things, and the last of all things. O God, send Thy Blessings upon his children, upon the women of his house, upon his descendents, upon his companions, and upon his group (which is) from among the Prophets, Messengers and Friends of God. O God, send Thy Blessings upon them all with Thy Mercy, O the Most Merciful of all.

NOTES

1. Qur'an: 68.1. The Arabic letter ن *(nun)* which sounds like the English letter N, is also a word meaning a fish, an inkpot, a well, or the trunk of a tree. Sufis refer by it to the mystery of Unicity *(ahadiyya)* and regard it as containing all cosmic and divine potentialities. It also symbolizes Divine Knowledge (Abdul Karim ibn Ibrahim al-Jili: *Insan'l-Kamil fi m'arifat'l- awakhir wa'l-awail*, 11.22.3). The treatise under review however seems to limit its significance:

و النون عبارة عن دائرة الكون

The letter Nun is the circle of the universe

2. Qur'an: 68.1; 96.4. A Symbol for the First Manifestation, the Intellect. For a profound and authoritative expression of this view of the Intellect, see Plotinus: The Enneads. Nasafi *(Insan'l-Kamil)* says: lbn Arabi *(Risalat'l Anwar fima yumnah sahib·al-khalwa min'l-asrar)* refers to the Mover of the Pen as the Right Hand of Truth, meaning the Attribute of Beauty *'Jamal'*). *Qalam* (Pen) is thereby a symbol of *'Aql* (Intellect).

3. Non-Qur'anic. It is derived from the root, *wajada*, which means 'he found'. As the root suggests, there is an association of the idea of self-discovery with the Arabic concept of existence *(wujud)*. *Afnan* (Philosophical Terminology in Arabic and Persian) refers to the difficulties of distinguishing between the concepts of being and existence. In theological discourse, however, *'dhat'* is accepted as an appropriate term for 'being' as distinct from *'sifat'* (attributes), as far as the philosophical discourse is concerned, we owe the distinction

between 'necessary' *(wajib)* and *'mumkin'* (contingent) being/existence to Ibn Sina. The *'mumkin'l-wujud'* is what Mirat'l-Arifin considers as "extant in God but non-existent by itself" *(maujud'n bihi wa madum'n bi naf-sihi).*

4. The verb *'aknaza'* is a reference to the well-known hadith Qudsi: "I was a hidden treasure" *(kanz).*

5. Non-Quranic. *'adum'* meaning non-existence, privation and nothingness refers to the unmanifested Being, or Being before Manifestation. The philosophical use is traceable from Kindi *(Rasa'il)* and Farabi *(Ara' Ahl'l-Madinat'l-fadhila).*

6. Qur'an: 3.7;13.39; 43.4

7. Qur'an: 85.22

8. Qur'an: 5.15; 6.59; 10.61; 11.6; 12.1

9. Qur'anic: 2.45. Qur'anic Categories: *'Nafs Ammara'* (12.53), *'Nafs Lawwama'* (75.2), and *'Nafs Mutma'inna'* (89.27). Major Qur'anic References on *Nafs*: Death associated with *Nafs* (3.185, 29.57.57); Jesus distinguishes between *'nafsi'* (my self) and *'nafsika'* (referring to God) 5.116; *Nafs* as place of *'zikr'* 7.205; *Nafs* as 'book' 17.14, 51.21, 41.53. The philosophical definition is:

> *The self is the source of all movements*
> (As from Nasir Khusraw in the book
> "Provision of the Travelers")

One of the earliest examples of comparison between *nafs* (self) and *'aql* (intellect) is found in Ibn Sina's Kitab'l-Nijat.

10. *'Aql* (Intellect) is Qur'anic not in form but in sense. The verbal form in the Qur'an, *Yaqilun* (16.57), meaning 'understanding' shares the semantic field with other Qur'anic concepts of *'ilm* (knowledge), *fikr* (reflec-

tion), and *zikr* (contemplation). See Rosenthal: The Triumphant Knowledge, the Concept of Ilm in Medieval Islam, and H. Askari: Society and State in Islam (Chapter on "Modes of Cognition in the Qur'an").

The origin of the term is a matter of immense importance for all disciplines of knowledge in Islamic thought. Abu Zaid al-Balqi *(Kitab al-Bad'a wa 'l-tarikh)* says:

قِيل سُمِّيَ عقل لأنه عُقال للمرء من التخطى لما خطر عليه

It was said that it had been called mind because it prevents a person from overstepping what comes to his mind

This meaning of *'aql* as something which binds, controls or prevents one from endangering himself is an explicit reference to what philosophers designate as the practical intelligence. As far as its Qur'a-nic and early Muslim connotations are concerned, lbn Taymiyya (Kitab al-Radd ala al-mantiqiyyin) says:

فالعقل فى لغة الرسول و أصحابه و أته عرض من الأعراض
يكون مصدر عَقَلَ عقلاً
و العقل فى لغة فلاسفة اليونان جوهر قائم بنفسه

In the language of the Messenger and his companions, the mind is an accident. The source of the verb 'aqala is 'aqlā.'
In the language of the Greek philosophers, the mind is an essence that exists on its own

lbn Taymiyya is categorical that in the usage of the Messenger and of his companions and community (*'aql*) was just the infinitive, "to understand" and (here he gives his own opinion) was an 'accident' *(aradh)* like any other 'accident' whereas in the usage of the philosophers of Greece (and their followers) it was a self-subsistent entity. lbn Taymiyya rejects the hadith regarding *'aql* being the first creation of God as 'fabricated':

أول ما خلق الله العقل حديث موضوع باتفاق اعمل المعرفة بالحديث

The first thing God created was the mind. A hadith that was fabri-cated by consensus. Work on knowledge through hadith

But the over-whelming evidence of the Muslim philoso-phers and mystics is in favour of the concept of Intel-lect in more or less Plotinian sense (see The Enneads). lbn Rushd *(Tahafut al-Tahafut)* defines the First Intellect as Pure Act and its own Cause: فعل محض و علته

Farabi *(Risa fi al-Aql)* regards the first Intellect as:

الموجود الأول و الواحد الأول و الحق الأول

The First Existent, the First One, and the First Reality

Kindi (Rasa'il) gives a standard philosophical definition:

The essence of everything is simple that understands everything as they are.

lbn Sina classifies it as Theoretical Reason *(nazri)*, Practi-cal Reason *(amali)*, and Material Reason *(hayulani)*. See his *Risa al-Hudud*. Nafasi *(Insanul Kamil)* goes to the extent of saying that Intellect is the Vicegerant of God. Both Fara-bi and lbn Sina, while referring to God, regard Him as

واجب الوجود بذاته عقل و عاقل و معقول

The necessary existence in Himself is mind, rational, and intelligible

The perspective on *'Aql* in Islamic thought could be summed up as follows: (a) Intellection - the act of rea-soning and understanding (as based on the original and 'apparent' Qur'anic form of the word), and (b) Intellect - an Existent which, in a theistic context, is the First Manifestation.

The treatise under review seems to forestall the defi-nition of *'Aql* as the Intellect but with a difference of far-reaching significance: it identifies the Intellect with the *Nafs'in wahida* (undivided self) of the Qur'an. Intellect now, unlike the Plotinian concept, is both a *nafs* (self) and also *wahid* (one). The *sirr* (secret) of *'Aql* is in its *wahdat* (unity). We cannot make things explicit here. Some of the aspects of this 'secret' will be touched upon at a later stage. For the present we just stress this point that Mirat'l-Arifin regards *'aql* as a creation, and as such it is extant in God but non-existent by itself. It is therefore not the self-subsistent entity which Ibn Taymiyya associates with the 'Greek philosophers'.

For controversies about the nature of *'aql* see al-Muhasibi's *Kitab Mahiyat'l-aql wa ma'anahu was ikhtilaf al-nas fihi* (MS. Carullah. No. 1101, Istanbul). See also R. A. Nicholson: Studies in Islamic Mysticism; M. Iqbal: The Development of Metaphysics in Persia; Seyyed Hossein Nasr: An Introduction to Islamic Cosmological Doctrines; and also his Gifford Lectures, Knowledge and the Sacred; and M. M. Sharif: The History of Muslim Philosophy, Vol. II.

11. Plural: Qur'an: 74.29.

12. Bukhari: I, Nikah 80; Muslim: 61, 62; Abu Da'ud: 35; Ibn Majah: 77; Hanbal: 2.498; 5, 8.

13. Qur'an: 4.1; 6.98; 7.189; 31.28; 39.6.

14. *'haba'*: 'motes' (Afnan: Philosophical Lexicon, Arabic and Persian). Lane (An Arabic-English Lexicon, Part 8 Book I, pp. 363-64): *habba* means (a star) rose. The meaning of 'rising' or 'blowing' (of the wind) is generally associated with the word. Ibn Arabi (Futuhat, Ch. 6): "When He (God) willed the existence of the world and its establishment in accordance with the determination of which He was aware through the knowledge which He had from Himself, from this entirely pure will there was produced a passive element, by a kind of

irradiation of Transcendence towards universal Reality; thus there was produced a reality known as *al-haba* (literally, a cloud of atoms). Then He irradiated with His Light towards this cloud, which the scholars call universal matter *(hayula)* and in which the whole world is in being." For details see under *hayula*.

15. If one accepts Afnan's view that *'hayula'* is a transcribed form of *hyle*, the term could have entered the Arabic language only after the Greek works had been translated. This would then be an unquestionable proof that at least the opening part of Mirat'l-A rifin could not be the work of Imam Husayn who lived long before the Greek works were available in Arabic. But it is not so easy to decide about the term under review, for that matter, any term. Those scholars who regard the philosophical vocabulary of the Arabs as largely derived from the translation of the Greek texts seem to ignore certain very important considerations.

(1) The translators were not building in a vacuum but on a widely established foundation which possessed the potential for abstract forms of expression. The very nature of the Arabic language allowed for deriving from one root both associated and differentiated sets of abstractions. One example will suffice here: *Haqq* meaning Reality/Truth is one of the most important concepts stressed in the Qur'an and was given therein a conceptual identity of far-reaching epistemological significance. This led to a terminology which was in no way indebted to the influence of the Greek translations but was present within the conceptual potential of the term, *Haqq*: one may list under it terms such as *'Haqqiqiyyah'*, *'Haqiqah'*, *'Haqiqat'*, *'al-Haqaiq' 'tahqiq'*, *'muhaqqiq' 'istehqaq'*. It is astonishing that Afnan speaks of "the almost total absence of abstractions in the language" (Philosophical Terminology, p. 32) and

sets aside the Qur'anic term, *rahbaniyya*, saying that it is not a concept but only a reference to the concrete practices of the monks. This is unacceptable because to judge which expression is a concept requires one to identify in which kind of discourse it is located; and it is obvious that one word could be either a concept, a metaphor or a concrete reference depending upon the discourse of which it is then a patt. Before deciding the question of discourse, one cannot pick up one term in isolation and pass judgement about its status. As a matter of fact, there is no general and uniform status for any word in human speech.

(2) If Ibn al-Muqaffa predates other translators, one should not merely ask on what foundations he is building his terminology but rigorously explore the structure of those foundations, their components, and the diversity of discourses. It is a deplorable tendency among modern scholars to undervalue the great semantic event, namely, the Qur'an. Thanks to the Japanese scholar, T. Izutsu, this has been considerably balanced and we can now appreciate the transformations which the Qur'an brought about in the structure of Arabic thought by lifting a concrete reference out of its empirical context and making it a concept or a metaphor to point to a general and transcendental level of reality. The revolution that the Qur'an created can be summed up as a movement from *tashbih* to *tanzih*, from the concrete to the abstract, which led to a diversity of discourse, literal, symbolic, and conceptual, culminating in at least four well known disciplines: *'kalam'* (theology), *'fiqh'* (jurisprudence), *'hikma'* (philosophy), and *'tasaw-wuf'* (mysticism). Before determining the status of a term, it is paramount to discover to which discourse it first belonged, whether it was a term of single discourse or multiple discourse.

(3) The Qur'an itself contains a multiple discourse, fold within fold, a *zahir* and a *batin*, from clear to "ambiguous" statements, from "signs" to parables. The response to the Qur'an also became a manifold. The foundations of this manifold were however laid in the nature of that *'ilm* which developed around the teachings of the Qur'an, for the Qur'anic knowledge was such that it asked for interpretation, *tawil*. The first hermeneutics of the Qur'an was developed by the children and the companions of Ali Ibn Abi Talib, and as the group was both suspected and persecuted, it was natural they should teach in a form that was indirect. Hence, we have in the teachings of the Imams a diversity of discourse - from *khutbat* to *munajat* (speeches and prayers) and within each form a further diversity of expression combining symbol with concept, metaphor with example, so that only those who knew what was really intended could understand their true meaning. If we find a term in their teachings, we should be extremely cautious because the *akhbar* (reports) concerning what they taught have reached us in fragments and in doctrinal forms. This is the case with Mirat'l-Arifin. There are many terms in it which appear to be of later origin. But it is quite probable that they were present earlier to the development of philosophical literature and had different connotations. The philosophical development, usually looked upon as a great movement that gave to the Arabic language a vast structure of abstract terminology, might have been in an other sense restrictive: it might have robbed a word of its vast symbolic value by turning it into a concept within a particular discourse. Such seems to be the case with the term, *hayula*.

The fact that the term was not restricted to one discourse is brought out by Tahanawi (2,1534).

AI-Kwarizmi *(Mafatih'l-Ulum)* gives the example of the discourse of the *hukuma* (philosophers).

The foregoing definition refers to the body *(jism)* as comprising matter *(hayula)* and form *(surat)*. Matter consists of المادة والعنصر و الطينة (matter, element, and clay)and form of الشكل و الهيئة و الصفة (shape, form and description) But as we examine the definition again, we notice another discourse intertwined with it. When Khwarizmi distinguishes between 'door' *(bab)* and 'doorness' *(babiyya)*, he is referring to the same term, *hayula*, and yet involving now a totally different discourse, an unexpected shift from 'physics' to metaphysics, from 'matter' and 'form' to 'ideas'. This is precisely what Tanahawi had in mind while referring to how the concept of *'hayula'* was understood in different discourses. Khwarizmi's reference to *'babiyya'* ('doorness') reveals the secret that the term means much more than what its usage in philosophy suggests. This is confirmed when al-Jili speaks of thought as the material *(hayula)* of the cosmos. It is true that the connotation of materiality is there linked up with the term but the material now referred to is not 'matter' consisting of but of thought, خيال.

There is another side to this kind of problem. The meaning we put into the word "matter" depends on three things: i) what sort of world outlook we have, materialistic or idealistic; ii) at what stage is our knowledge of the material foundations of things; and iii) in what particular discourse we are engaged when we use the term in question. What is obvious is that as far as knowledge of the material world is concerned we are now far from the simplistic and erroneous conception of the well-known four elements - air, fire, earth, talk about matter is to first determine at what level we are looking at it - molecular, atomic, nuclear, sub-nuclear. But the surprising thing about the words we use is that we can all pretend to carry on a meaningful conversation by sharing a word though it is understood quite differently by each one of us. A mystic, a nuclear physicist, a Marxist, and a brickmaker can all use the word, matter, for at least a few minutes, if such a group could be imagined as carrying on some kind of talking, if for no other reason than that they are all members of the human race. But very soon all communication between them will stop as soon as they discove that they do not really understand each other. But when each member of our extraordinary group returns to his own associates, the word that was previously a sheer fiction obtains a meaningfulness within the discourse which is the universe of his thought. Hence, when we hear somebody speaking, we should know who he is; for to communicate we need some insight into his being. When he is a mystic and when he says *'hayula'* from which the form of the universe was brought out, we cannot possibly draw from his referenc to *'hayula'* that he is speaking of matter in a physical sense because being a mystic he knows that the real agent is Formative Thought, or in the Qur'anic terms, the *'amr'* of God. In order to hint at what he really means by *'hayula'* he may bring in close juxtaposition another word about whose status there is no confusion, namely, *'anqa'* (see Note 16), that it is a fabulous bird "whose name is known but whose body is not known" and that it is a symbol. To bring it into an equation with a concept, namely, *hayula*, is to hint at the true meaning of both, that the reference is to a reality whose name is known but whose body is not known. This device of juxtaposing concepts and symbols is familiar to students of mystical texts because this is one of the ways in which true meanings are both concealed and expressed. In the text of the treatise under review we read about five things - *haba* (see Note 14) which means 'blowing mist' or 'cloud of atoms' (concrete reference); *hayula* which is a concept for 'matter'. *'anqa* which is a fabulous bird (a symbolic reference); which means 'a patched garment' (most probably another symbolic hint); and *'unsur'* which means 'element' (both concept and a concrete reference). Such an extraordinary combination cannot be meaningless nor just there for the most of words. See Note 18 for our interpretation of *'unsur'*. What is suggested here is that in the context in which *'hayula'* I mentioned it cannot possibly mean 'matter' as it was understood by the philosophers. It was a reference to a reality whose nature was revealed through the symbolism of 'bird' and 'patched garment'. Those who are familiar with this mode of communication are not deceived by the apparent meaning of a term. For example, *haba* is meant to represent 'a cloud of atoms'. But Abu Yusuf Afzaluddin, one of the Khalifas of Khaja Hasan Nizami of Delhi, while referring to this term in his Urdu translation of Mirat'l-Arifin, says that it is "the outward of the Spirit which has the potentiality to manifest the forms of the world."

It appears that both Ibn Arabi and al-Jili tend to go into details about the first irradiation *(tajalli)* and refer to the terms we have discussed here as if they are physical realities. But one should make oneself familiar with the totality of their writings in order to apprehend how far their reference is 'physical'.

16. It "signifies a bird, of which the name is known but the body is not known (or it is a fabulous bird) ... it is said to mean a great bird that is not seen save once in ages; and by frequency of usage it became a name for calamity ... it is also said to be called *('anqa)* because it has on its neck a whiteness like the neck-ring ... it is found at the place of the setting of the sun." (Lane: An Arabic-English Lexicon, Part 5 Book 1, p. 2177.)

The difficulty is that *('anqa)* is a symbol here and is identified with *'hayula'* which is a concept, and with *'haba'*
which literally means 'blowing' or perhaps blowing mist.

17. Qur'anic: 82.8. It is a well-defined term in philosophy:
Farabi
(Mafariqat): الصورة الجسمية لمتخيلة و المحسوسة و المتوهمة
(The physical image of the imaginary, the tangible and
the delusioned)
Ibo Sina *(Kitab'l-Nijat)*:صورة سارية متفارقة معقولة جسمية
(Material, separate, intelligible and corporal forms)
Ghazali *(Maqasid)*: الصورة عند المتكلمين عرض تابع الوجود و
المحل (According to the speakers, the image is the dis-
play of existence, and location is dependent)

18. Non-Qur'anic. According to Lane (Arabic-English
Lexicon, Part III, Book I, p. 1027), *'rataqa'* means 'he
sewed up'; *'ritaq'* means a 'patched garment' or a garment of two pieces of cloth sewed together; and there
are other meanings which are not relevant here. Now,
'ratq' is identified in the text with the great element -
'unsur'l-azam.

The scientific meaning in the conventional language
of philosophy is that of an element whereof are composed the material substances of different natures. But
Lane (part 5, p. 2063) gives another meaning of *'unsur*:

فلان كريم العنصر

Such a one is of generous origin, or race.

And if we apply this meaning to the present text, *'unsur'l-azam* will mean 'the great origin' (not the 'element'
of philosophy). This is another proof that the terms
used in Mirat'l-Arifin possess meanings which are different from what the terms came to mean in philosophical discourse. And as for this 'great origin' Suharwardi
(Hikmat'l-Ishraq) says:

العقل المسمى بالعنصر الأعلى

The mind called the supreme element

and Mulla Sadruddin Shirazi *(Rasa'il)* adds:

فى لسان الفلسفة بالعنصر الأعلى و فى لسان الشريعة بالقلم الأعلى الإلهى

In the language of philosophy, by the highest element, and in the language of Shari'a, by the highest divine pen

19. *'ayan*: individual, entity, essence. Non-Qur'anic in sense. Afnan says that "it is difficult to tell how and when it first originated" (Philosophical Terminology, p.101). Sayuti (Al Muzhir. Vol i. p.459) defines

العين نفس الشىء

'ayan is exactly the same thing

Other definitions are:
lbn al-Muqaffa *(Mantiq)*:

عين الشىء أصله

The *'ayan of the thing is its origin*

Mulla Sadra *(Asfar)*:

المسماة بالمهيات عند الحكماء و بالأعيان الثابتة عند أرباب الكشف

Called the essences by the wise men and the fixed entities by the masters of revelation

It is significant that while translating the first of the Aristotlean Categories lbn Muqaffa uses the term *('ayan)*, whereas Kindi, Dimishqi, the Ikhwan al-Safa, and lbn Sina translate it as جَوْهَر *(essence)*. The latter regards it as contrary to عَرَض *(accident)*.

20. In philosophical discourse, it means 'generated bodies', also it is a general term for world/cosmos. The plural however suggests that the term stands for 'body';

and hence, lbn Sina *(Kitab al-Nijat)* speaks of نظام الأكوان
(The system of the universes), and Jami *(Sharah Attar)*
refers to مراقب كونى (Cosmic observer). But later in
Mirat'l-Arifin we get the abstraction, *kauniyya*, and this
will then mean Cosmic/phenomenal.

21. Qur'an: 52.2

22. Qur'an: 52.2; 17.58; 33.6

23. Qur'anic: 22.11 meaning 'margin' which is not relevant
here. The plural in the text means 'letters'.

24. Qur'anc: 10.64; 18.109; 7.158; 18.27; 66.12.

25. See the Introduction.

26. Fatiha meaning 'opening' is the title of the first chapter of the Qu-r'an, Fatiha as "the Seven Oft-Repeated
Verses" (Qur'an 15.87).

27. The reference is not clear. It is not certain whether it
refers to the Prophet who is later designated as 'Word',
or is an obvious reference to the Greatest Name of
God. Abu Da'ud (Bab al-Witr 23) gives the following
hadith:

اسم الله الأعظم فى هاتين الآيتين
و فاتحة الكتاب و آل عمران

The greatest name of God is in these two verses
and the Opening of the book and Al 'Imran

The Opening of Al-'lmran (Chapter 3 of the Qur'an):

ٱللَّهُ لَآ إِلَٰهَ إِلَّا هُوَ ٱلْحَىُّ ٱلْقَيُّومُ ۝

- mentions 'the Greatest Name', The Living, the Ever Lasting.

28. The importance of Fatiha is clearly established on
the basis of Prophetic Tradition: Tirmidhi: Mawaqit
63; Hanbal: 2, 428; Bukhari: Jana'z 66; Tirmidhi: Jana'iz 39; reference is also made in the Tradition to the

Fatiha of the Torah: Al Darimi, Fadhail Qur'an 1.7. The beginning of Torah is An'am, and its end is Hud. Fakhruddin Razi's commentary on Fatiha, Sadruddin Qunawi's *I'Jaz'l-Bayan fi ta'wil Ummi'l-Qur'an*, and Abdul Karim Jili's exegesis of *Bismillah* are some of the old examples of the discussion on the importance of the Fatiha.

Abul Kalam Azad's detailed commentary after the approach of Mohammad Abduh is however a different attempt. Also refer to Tabari: 1.35-66; Zamakshari: Kashshaf 1-15; and Sayuti: Itkan 1.54.

29. Title of Ali ibn'l-Husayn, the fourth Imam of the Shi'ites.

30. Qur'an: 2.119; 7.54; 14.32; 16.77; 17.85.

31. Qur'an: 3.190; 13.16; 30.11

32. *'Harr'* is here a representation of both the status of a thing and also a reference to hos we look at it. For an esoteric reflection on the mystery of *'harf'*, see al-Niffari: Mawaqif (tr. A. J. Arberry)

33. A Qur'anic Concept: 'Common word' 3.64; 'Pure Word' 14.24; 'Word of God' 9.40; 'His Word' - John and Jesus 3.39, 3.45, 4.171, 7.137, 9.40; Word of Piety 47.26; Lasting Word 43.28; As Decree/Judgement 10.19, 33.96, 11.110, 119; 20.129, 39.19, 71; 40.6; 41.45, 42.14; 42.21; 'True Word' 6.115; *'Qual'* (Utterance) 9.74, 18.5; *'Kalimat'* (for Adam, Abraham) 2.37, 2.124, 66.12; Unchangeable Word 6.34, 10.64; Countless Words 18.109, 31.27, 18.27.

34. This is a reference to those letters which are found in the Qur'an at the beginning of certain chapters about which there are several theories (Refer to Bell and Watt: Introduction to the Qur'an, and also to "Letter Symbolism in Sufi Literature" in A. Schimmel's The

Mystical Dimensions of Islam). Mirat'l-Arifin contains certain principles to decode these mystery letters by giving one example of *'Alif Lam Mim'*, the letters with which the second chapter of the Qur'an begins.

This is how the mystery letters are located in the Qur'an:
1) الم (Chapters 2, 3, 29, 30, 31, 32)
2) المص (Chapter 7)
3) المر (Chapter 13)
4) الر (Chapters 10, 11, 12, 14, 15)
5) كهيعص (Chapter 19)
6) طه (Chapter 20)
7) طسم (Chapter 26, 28)
8) طس (Chapter 27)
9) يس (Chapter 36)
10) ص (Chapter 38)
11) حم (Chapters 40, 41, 42, 43, 44, 45, 46)
12) ق (Chapter 50)
13) ن (Chapter 68)

35. A compound expression is one which is composed of two or more words. Example: *athna'ashr* (twelve).

36. Qur'an: 2.23; 9.64; 9.86; 9.124; 9.127; 10.38; 24.1.

37. Non-Qur'anic. The philosophical use of *wajhah*:

وجيه عقلى وجيه كونى

Wise, rational and cosmic

(Mulla Sadra: *Afsar*)

38. Qur'anic in form but not in sense. It has different connotations among philosophers and theologians. Ibn Sina *(kitab al Nijat)* defines it as follows:

كل ذات قوامها فهو عَرَض

Every being has its own structure, is an accident

See also Ghazali: معيار (p. 171)

39. Non-Qur'anic. *Luzum/liwazim* mean concomitant/s. Ibn Sina *(Kitab Mantiq al-Mashriqayn)* says:

لازم يوصف الشىء بعد تحقق ذاته

The thing must be described after it has been realized

40. N*isba* is relation - causal, biological, logical, and spiritual. *Madhaf* means 'the correlative' which Ibn Sina *(Danish Name Ala'i)* defines as to add an attribute is its quality, so that everything can be compared with the other.

41. If *Haqq* has many different connotations in the Qur'an. Here it refers to God as the Ultimate Truth and Reality (Qur'an: 22.6; 24.25) Mulla Sadra *(Afsar)* says, in his characteristic manner, about God that He is the Truth of all truths, the Ability of all atoms and the Essence of all essences.

42. "He was and there was nothing beside Him. He is as He was." It was one of those Prophetic sayings which, though not found in the traditional collections of hadith, led to a profound and extensive development of Sufi thought. "He is as He was" is one of the few statements in the history of religious literature which sum up a world of mystery. We can only refer here to its most obvious meaning that God is such that nothing was added to Him when the worlds came into existence and He will not be made less by their passing away

43. D*hat* as Kindi *(Rasa'il)* defines it as ذات الشىء which means 'essence of a thing'. Similar is its use as a term in Farabi *(Madinat al-fadhila)*, Ibn Sina *(Kitab al-Nijat)*, and Ibn Rushd *(Tahafut al-Tahafut)*. According to Sayuti *(Al Muzhir)*, its use began by the *Mutakallemin*. Among the philosophers it began with Kindi.

44. '*Ilm* (knowledge) and *dhat* (Being) are one. Nasir Khusraw *(Zad al-Musafirin)* says: Divine knowledge is self-knowledge.

The unity of *dhat* and *sifat* as a well-known theological postulate of the *Mu'tazalites* only resembles the reference then to the oneness of knowledge and Being. We can only tell in terms of a metaphor - a mirror which helps us to apprehend (not conceive) the transparent nature of *'ilm* in relation to *dhat*.

The Muslim preoccupation with knowledge both philosophically and religiously is based on the Qur'anic concern with the *furqan* between truth and untruth. The Qur'an contains theory of knowledge which requires to be fully explored. The references to (a) ريب (b) شبه (c) شك (d) ظن (e) علم and (f) يقين constitute a system (Qur'an: 4.171).

The *'ilm*, in this series, should not be confused with God's *'ilm* for His knowledge does not involve a preceding state of doubt and a following state of certitude. Hence, *'ilm* in the series, enlisted here is *ma'arifa*, and it is precisely this *ma'arifi* which is one of the themes of Mirat'l-Arifin.

See Izutsu: *A Comparative Study of Key Philosophir, Concepts in Sufism and Taoism; Seyyed Hossein Nasr Knowledge and the Sacred;* M. M. Sharif: *History of Muslim, Philosophy,* Vol II.

45. The Divine Realities *(haqaiqa ilahiyya)* pertain to knowledge emanating from God for which there are two manifestaions - *Umm'l-kitab* which is knowledge in its totality a generality, and *Kitab'l-Mubin* which is knowledge in unfolding into details and particulars. The former stands for *dhat* (Being) wherein there is no differentiation, and hence the totality and generality which *Umm'l-Kitab* represents is linked with *Dhat*, whereas Knowledge, as a movement from the general to the particular, is linked with *Kitab'l-Mubin* which by definition is a Detailed Book. Knowledge of God is

however one, and its Godly character is not at all affected whether we call it by one name or many names. This is similar to what al-Jili *(Insan'l Kamil)* says of the *Ruh* (The Spirit) which has many names - The Pen, the Spirit of Muhammad, the First Intelligence, and the Holy Spirit, on the principle of naming the original by the derivation, but in the presence of God it has only one name, *al-Ruh*. The same thing can be said about *'Ilm* and its different names.

46. The Cosmic (phenomenal) Realities *(haqaiq kauniyya)* appear to pertain to the embodiment of knowledge in the Pen and the Tablet. But this stage is far from 'embodiment' except that the images of the Pen and the Tablet seem to refer to this principle. The dimensions of thought involved here are far from a simple difference between a Pure idea and an Image. Even in the descent *(tanazzul)* of *'Ilm* there is always the link with the transcendental. Therefore, Mirat'l-Arifin im-mediately adds that there is correspondence between *Qalam* (Pen) and *Dhat* (Being).

47. Qur'an: 2.251; 3.26; 5.17

48. Qur'an: 38.34; 20.5

49. Qur'an: 2.255; 38.34

50. Abdul Karim al-Jili *(Insan'l Kamil)* uses the same expression - *nuskha* (copy, transcript). There is an overall correspondence between al-Jili's *Insan'l Kamil* and Mirat'l Arifin but the latter is a compact and systematic essay with an authority of an Imam. Mirat'l-Arifin can be regarded as *umm'l kitab* for whatever has been written afterwards about the Fatiha and *Insan'l Kamil*. See the Introduction for details.

51. The earliest reference to the idea of a Perfect Man is made by Abu Yazid al-Bastami (d.874), a contempo-

rary of Imam Hasan al-Askari (d.872), who defines "the perfect and complete man" (al-kamilu'l-ta-mm) who, after being invested with Divine attributes, becomes unconscious of them. This definition of "the perfect and complete man" is cited by Abul Qasim al-Qushairi (d.1074) in his famous *Risala* (p.140, 1.12). Also refer to the *Sharah Risala-i Qushairiyya* by the sixth Chishti Saint, Khaja Gesuderaz of Gulbarga (d. 1442); Ibn Miskawaih: *Faudh al-Asghar*; Ghazali: *Mishkat al Anwar*, and *Ihya'Ulum al-Din*, Vol IV; Suharwardi Muqtul: *Munis'l-Ush'shaq*; *Rasa'il Ikhwan al-Safa* Part III; Ibn Arabi: *Fusus al-Hikam*, *Futuhat al-Makkaiyya*, and *al tadbirat al-ilahiyya fi islah al-mumlikat al-insaniyya*; Ibn Kadib al-Bari: *Mawakif al-ilahiyya*; Abdul Karim al-Jili: *al insan'l-kamilfi ma'ifati'l awakhir wa'l-awa'il*; and Mahmud Shabistari: *Gulshan-i Raz*.

Also Abdul Jabbar al-Niffari: *Mawakhif*; Fariddudin Attar: Tadh*kirat al-auliya* and *Mantiq at-tayr*; Ali Ibn Uthman al-Hujwiri: *Kashf al-Mahjub*; Abu'l Majd Majdud Sana'i: *Hadiqat al-haqiqat wa shari'at at-tariqat*; Abdurrahman Jami: *Nafahat al-uns*; Jalaluddin Rumi: *Mathnawi*; Abu Nasr as-Sarraj: *Kitab al-luma fi 'l tasawwuf*; Khaja Mir Dard: *'Ilm'l-Kitab*.

For the *Tafsir* of Imam Jafar al-Sadiq see Paul Nwyia: Exegese coranique at langage mystique.

For modern works: M. Iqbal: *The Development of Meta physics in Persia*; Louis Massignon: *La passion d'al-Hosayn ibn Mansour al-Hallaj*; R. A. Nicholson: Studies in Islamic Mysticism; Henri Corbin: *L'Homme de lumiere dans le soufisme iranien*; and also Corbin's Creative Imagination of Ibn Arabi; M. M. Sharif: *The History of Muslim Philosophy*; and Seyyed Hossein Nasr: *An Introduction to Islamic Cosmological Doctrines*, and *Knowledge and the Sacred*; T. Izutsu: *A Comparative Study of the Key Philosophical Concepts of Sufism and Taoism*; E. Underhill: Mysticism: *A Study in*

the Nature and Development of Man's Spiritual Consciousness;
F. Schuon: *Dimensions of Islam*; and A. Schimmel: *The Mystical Dimensions of Islam*.

For the development of the idea of *insan'l-kamil* see the Introduction.

We should, however briefly, list here the most central forms of expression used in the Islamic literature to describe or refer to the Perfect Man.

1)   "The Perfect and complete man" *(al-kamilu'l-ta'mm)* Bayazid al-Bastami.
2)   "The Microcosm" *('alum 'l-saghir)* - *Ikhwan'l-Safa*, and *Ibn Miskawaih*
3)   "The all-inclusive world" *(kaun jamai)* - Ibn Arabi.
4)   "The middle world" or "the all-comprehensive middle" *(barzakh jamai)* - Abdul Karim al-Jili
5)   "The Mirror" *(mirat)* - Abdul Karim al-Jili

Forms of expression which are derived from the Qur'an and applied to the Perfect Man are: The Vicegerant of God *(khalifa't-allah)*; *'kalima'* (Word); The Manifest Imam *(Imam'l-mubin)*; and "One with whom is the knowledge of the Book" *(Sura 13, last verse)*.

The titles by which the Perfect Man is called are: *Imam* (among *Shi'ites*), *Qutb* (Pole), *Madar* (Pivot), *Wali* (Saint) and *Shaykh* (Master) in *Sunni* circles.

Mirat'l-Arifin takes the concept to the level of *haqiqat'l kulliyyat'l-insaniyya* (Totality of the Human Reality) with the equation between the Fatiha of the *Kitab* and *Insan'l-Kamil* who includes both the cosmic and spiritual realities and is a *barzakh* between them.

52. T*a'yyun*: in individuation/specification

التعين هو الشخص
و التعين الأول عند الصوفية هو مرتبة الوحدة
و التعين الثانى مرتبة الوحدانية

*The designation is the person. And, the first designation for Sufis is
the level of unity. The second designation is the level of Oneness*

53. H*ulul*: transmigration/descending upon/incarnation.
Nasafi in Insanul Kamil says:

حلول و اتحاد باطل شد

الحلول نوعين: حلول صفات غير مدركة و صفات مدركة

*Solutions and invalid union are two types of solutions:
solutions of intangible attributes and solutions of
tangible attributes*

54. S*huhud* is not a philosophic term. *Mutluq* is defined by
Jami *(Sharah Attar)* as *ghair muqqaiyad* (unconditioned).
Shuhud however is an important Sufi term associated
with the doctrine of *wahdat al-shuhud* (unity of contemplation). In strictly doctrinal terms, those who follow
the school of *wahdat al-wujud* regard divine attributes as
'ayn dhat (one with Being, Being itself), whereas those
who are *shuhudi* regard Divine attributes neither Being
nor other than Being.

55. Qur'an: 30.7; 57.3; and 57.13.

56. Qur'anic. *Balin*: 57.3 Pl. *Butun*. The Qur'anic usage of
the plural, except in the case of 16.69 which allows
reflection on its metaphorical aspect, is not related to
the concept in the treatise under review.

57. B*arzaq*. Qur'an: 23.100; 25.53; and 55.20. It occurs in
Suharwardi's *Ishraq*, Jami's *Sharah Attar*, and Mulla Sadra's *Asfar*. Abdul Karim al-Jili says: "The Perfect man
is neither Absolute Being nor contingent being but a
third metaphysical category *(barzaq)* - cited in Nicholson's *Studies of Islamic Mysticism*, p. 104.

58. Qur'an (In connection with Jesus - the Holy Spirit):
2.87; 2.253; 5.110; Spirit from Him, 4.171; in connection with Mary, 19.17, 21.91; 66.12; *Gabriel as Ruh*

al-Amin, 26.193; in connection with Adam, 32.9; 15.29; 38.72; and as *Amr*, 17.85.

59. Mirat'l-Arifin follows the Qur'anic distinction between *Ruh* (Spirit) and *Nafs* (Self).

60. For a recent emphasis on this perspective on man see Seyyed Hossein Nasr's *Knowledge and the Sacred* (Edinburgh University Press, 1981), particularly the chapters on "Man, Pontifical and Promothean" and "The Cosmos as Theophany".

61. "Who knows his self knows his Lord" - a hadith attributed to the Prophet and also to Ali Ibn Abi Talib whose authenticity is established by *tawatur* (unbroken oral transmission) written down in almost all Sufi texts. It is, however, not found in the traditional collections of hadith. Rumi (d.1273), like all other Sufis, refers to it in his Mathnawi. For its documentation see B. Furuzanfar's *Ahadith e Mathnawi* cited by A. Schimmel in *The Triumphal Sun*. It is only in the treatise under review that this celebrated saying forms part of a coherent system of thought, and only through this treatise that we realize in what framework the knowledge of the self is located. Also refer to Ibn Arabi's *Risala Wujudiya*.

62. 1) ديوان سيدنا على ابن أبى طالب (British Museum No. 14573.c.28)
2) ديوان شعر أمير المؤمنين على ابن أبى طالب (British Museum No. 14573.b.39) All the manuscripts (see Introduction) give the same verses as found in the text we have used here; except that in Manuscript (2) the order is different.

63. Qur'an:17.14.

64. Qur'an: 41.53.

65. Qur'an: 51.21.

66. 2.1.

67. A*hadiyya* (Unicity) as an Islamic way of referring to the Absolute Being rests for its authority on Qur'an 112. God is One, and to say this is not to bring Him under the category of number, as He transcends all predictions and all categories. *Ahadiyya* is a stage above *wahidiyya* (oneness). It is Pure Being, Unmanifested and Simple admitting of neither duality within nor without.

68. *Kaun Jamai* (a world comprehensive of all worlds) is Man - an idea found in *Rasa'il Ikhwan al-Safa*:

رسائل إخوان الصفا: جزء ثالث: الرسالة الثانية عشر من الجسميات
الطبيعيات في قول الحكماء: إن الإنسان عالم صغير
جزء ثالث: الرسالة الثالثة: إن العالم إنسان كبير

Epistles of the Brethren of Purity: Part Three: The Twelfth Epistle on the Corporeals Physical Studies on the Sages' Saying: Man is a Small World
Part Three: The Third Epistle: The World is a Large Human

Al-Jili advances the idea of the Brethren of Purity by stressing that the Perfect Man is a microcosmos of a higher order reflecting both the powers of nature and the Divine powers as in a mirror.

69. Qur'an: 13.43.

70. Qur'an: 6.59

71. Qur'an: 6.75; 7.185; 23.88; and 36.83.

72. The Perfect Man here is the Prophet.

73. Note: Mirat'l-Arifin refers to the *wahdat* (oneness) of Man and not to *ahadiyaa* (unicity) which should be said only of God.

74. The Arabic, *taur*, as a philosopic term means 'state' on the authority of Ibn Rushd *(Tahafut)*:

الموجود ينتقل من طور إلى طور

The existent moves from one phase to another

It is also worth noting that *al-maujud* here is the *mumkunul wujud* which is a term coined by lbn Sina to refer to 'contingent existence'.

Daur - meaning 'cycle' is classified by Ibn Taimiyya *(Kitab al-Radd ala al-mantaqiyan)* as

الدور ثلاثة الكونى الحكمى و الفقهى الحسابى

The role of the three: cosmic, legal, jurisprudential, and mathematical

75. *'mawatin'* (مواطن): Realms; singular: *'mawtin'* (موطن). Ibn Arabi refers by this term to the ultimate grounds or homelands of created experience. They are six in number: pre-creation, this world, the subtle (intermediate) world, Resurrection, Hell/Paradise, and the site of the Vision of God. The idea of *'mawtin'* (country/homeland) is also associated with the Sufi idea of 'moment': the 'moment' you are in is your 'country' or homeland. See Ibn Arabi's *Journey to the Lord of Power* (Tr. by Rabia Terri Haris, East West Publications, 1981)

76. Qur'an: 95.4; 17.70; 2.34.

77. Qur'an: 25.45.

78. One of the well-known *hadith qudsi* regarded as authentic by all Sufi schools. See William A. Graham: *Divine Word and Prophetic Word in Early Islam*, Monton, 1977.

79. Mirat'l-Arifin gives four categories of *Umm'l-kitab*:
    a) The point of the letter, *ba*;
    b) The *ba* of the *Bismillah*;
    c) The *Bismillah*; and
    d) The entire Fatiha.

80. A well-known conception associated with the *Ikhwan al-Safa*. See Geo Widengren's *The Gnostic Technical Language in the Rasa'il Ikhwan al-Safa*. Ibn Miskawaih *(Faudh al-Asghar Part III)* refers to Man both as a microcosm

and a composite: "Whatever things are found in the macrocosm are also found in man, both manifestly and obscurely. Man is composite. It is not possible for simple elements to be found in him in their simplicity because if that were so the simples would immediately dissolve man and cause him to be non-existent; if the fiery element came into the body in its simplicity it would burn up the other parts which were in the body, and all those parts would dissolve and find their centre. Thus all the elements are found in man in composition."

81. The technical definition of the point is given by lbn Sina (*Risalat'l-hudud*) as:

النقطة ذات غير مستقيمة و لها وضع هى نهاية الخط

*A point with a non-straight line and a position
is the end of a line*

But in the language of the mystics it is the last of the images from the world of phenomena to point to a world which neither a concept nor a symbol can represent. The Point is a hint of the Unmanifested and a symbol for the epitome of all existence and knowledge. It is without any quality and quantity and yet all qualities and quantities have emerged out of it. The point is there, and yet not there: it is a subtle *(latif)* existence which is also non-existence. It is called nothingness, and yet it is the beginning of all existence. The point is Existence; the line is extension and multiplicity; parallel lines are the origin and the end; and the circle is the falling back of everything on the One who is both present and absent.

82. The Arabic letter, *'sin'* (س) which sounds like the English, 's'.

83. Muslim 4.38, *isnad* 13 (Abu Huraira).
    Muslim 4.41, *isnad* 13; 4.39, *isnad* 24; 4.40, *isnad* 24.
    Musnad 11.241, *isnad* 13; 11.285, *isnad* 24; 11.460, *isnad* 24.
    Tirmidhi: *Tafsir* S.I. No. 1., *isnad* 13.
    Muwatta' 3.99, *isnad* 24.
    Nasai 11.23, *isnad* 24.
    Abu Da'ud: 2.132. *isnad* 24.

84. *Thalathan* could also mean "three times (Muhammad said)".

85. Ibn Majah: 33.52.6, *isnad* 13; the frame story is omitted.

86. Man as *'barzakh jamai'* (all-comprehensive mediator) is an idea which runs through all mystical literature. Abdul Karim al-Jili, as Nicholson says, regards man as cosmic thought "assuming flesh and connecting absolute Being with the world of nature." *(Studies in Islamic Mysticism, p.84)* Ibn Arabi *(al-Isfar 'an risalt'l anwar)* seems to restrict the concept of *'barzakh'* to his 'third realm' which is between this world and next. But he also calls it 'interval' and says that it is the imagination. Al-Tahanawi *(Istilahat)* reports (cited by R. Arnaldez, *"Insan al-Kamil"* Encylopaedia of Islam, Vol III, New Edition): "The Perfect Man is the isthmus *(barzakh)* between necessity *(wujub)* and possibility *(imkan)*, the mirror which combines the attributes of eternity and its laws with the attributes of the generation of beings. He is the central point between the *'Haqq'* and *'Khalqq'*. Through him and through his heirarchical rank *(martaba)*, the emanation *(fayd)* of the *haqq* and its presence *(madad)*, the source of subsistence *(baqa')* of that which is not God, make their way to the entire world, the upper and the lower. Without him (Man) and without the quality of *'barzakh' (barzakhiyya)* which does not cut itself off in either of the two extremes, nothing in the world would receive the divine pres-

ence of the Unique, for lack of relationship and link."
Al-Tahanawi also refers to Djami's *Sharh al-Fusus*
which also reiterates the same things about the Perfect
Man. Another passage from the article of Arnaldez
will bring out the development of the idea of *'barzakh'*
into that of a *qutb* and *madar* (pole and pivot). While
referring to Ibn Kadib al-Bari, Arnaldez says: "Man is
the point of the sphere which serves as a pivot *(madar)*
for existence. The Perfect Man is unique in all eternity.
But he appears in different guises *(malabis)* and receives
various names. His name in principle is Muhammad,
his *kunya Abu'l-Qasim*, his attribute *'Abd Allah*, his title
Shams al Din. His other names vary with each epoch,
in harmony with the guise of that epoch. But all are
united in Muhammad. Spiritual men are in the image
of Muhammad, which refers to the Muhammadan Reality, and one sees Muhammad in such images. There
is no metempsychosis *(tanasukh)* there, but merely the
irradiation *(tajalli)* of the Muhammadan Reality in each
era upon the most perfect of men, who thus become
the representatives *(khulafa)* of the Prophet on the
plane of manifestation *(zahir)*, while the Muhammadan
Reality is the hidden side of their own reality."

How far this doctrine is present in Mirat'l-Ari.fin see in
the Introduction, but for the moment we point out just
this that the treatise under review systematically moves
from the idea of *insan al-kamil* to *haqiqat al-kulliyyat'l-insaniyya*.

87. Qur'an: 55.27; 55.78.

88. Qur'an: 16.6 (which is not at the same conceptual level
as in the treatise under review). The Qur'anic conjunc-
tion of *Jamal* (beauty) with *sabr* (patience) and *Haqq*
(truth) is far more significant (12.18, 63; 73.18; 103).

89. *Kamal* (Perfection) is not a Qur'anic word but its con-

ception is spread over the entire Qur'an, for all the Beautiful Names of God reflect Perfection.

90. Qur'an: 7.48.

91. The starting point of all speculation concerning *ama* or *amayya* is the Prophetic Tradition: The Prophet was asked, "Where was your Lord before the creation of the world?" He replied, "In *ama*". All further knowledge about it is withheld. The author of the *Mirat'l-Arifin* also does not offer any clues. The hint is however made that to enter into discussion about it might lead us away from *tawhid*. But the speculation went on. *Arna* means 'blindness' and also 'cloud'. Ibn Arabi whose speculations could hardly be matched by any other mystical writer, whose ideas were explained by Abdul Karim al-Jili, identifies *ama* with the seat of the Name, *al-Rabb* (the Lord). The Prophet is reported to have added, "There was no space either above or below *(ama)*, which led to identify it as the dark mist above which is a void and below which is a void. However, the idea of *ama* proved useful to refer to the Unmanifested, the absolute inwardness *(butun)* or occulta- tion *(istitar)* of Reality, and Jili goes to the extent of putting *amayya* above *ahadiyya*. Here Jili goes beyond 'the One' of Plotinus. Let us recall here what a modern Muslim philosopher and mystic, Muhammad Iqbal, says in this connection: "We have now finished all the essential names and attributes of God, and proceed to examine the nature of what existed before all things." The Arabian Prophet, says al-Jili, was once questioned about the place of God before creation. He said that God, before the creation, existed in *'Arna'* (blindness). It is the nature of this blindness or primal darkness which we now proceed to examine. The investigation is particularly interesting, because the word translated into modern psychology would be 'the unconsciousness'.

This single word impresses upon us the farsightedness with which he anticipates the metaphysical doctrines of modern Germany. He says that the Unconsciousness is the reality of all realities; it is the Pure Being without any descending movement; it is free from the attributes of God and creation; it does not stand in need of any name or quality, because it is beyond the sphere of relation. It is distinguished from the absolute oneness because the latter name is applied to the Pure Being in its process of coming down towards manifestation. It should however be remembered that when we speak of the priority of God and the posteriority of creation, our words must not be understood as implying time; for there can be no duration of time or separateness between God and His creation. Time, continuity in space and time, are themselves creations, and how can a piece of creation intervene between God and His creation. Hence, our words before, after, where, whence, etc., in this sphere of thought, should not be construed to imply time or space. The real thing is beyond the grasp of human conceptions; no category of material existence can be applicable to it; because, as Kant would say, "the laws of phenomena cannot be spoken of as obtaining in the sphere of noumena." (Muhammad Iqbal: *The Development of Metaphysics in Persia*. Luzac, London 1908).

For the rejection of the hadith about *'amayya'* (عَمَائِيَة) as fabricated see a brief manuscript in India Office Library IOL Persian.

92. *'Bismillah'* occurs in the body of the text of the Qur'an three times: 1.1; 11.41;27.30

93. Qur'an: 31.27.

Appendix

Ahl'l-'Irfan Contemporaries of the Imams from the House of the Prophet

632-870-940
Ahl'l-'Irfan

IMAMS

1. Ali Ibn Abi Talib (d.41/661)	Abu Dhar Ghafari (d33/653) Salman al-Parisi (36/656) Muhammad b. Abu Bakr (38/658) Abu Darda 'Uwaym b. 'Amir(?) Uwaiys al-Qarani (40/660) Bilal Habashi Miqdad b. al-Aswad(?) Abu'l-Yaqzan 'Ammar b. Yasir(?) Ma'itham Tammar (?) Kumayl ibn Ziyad Najafi (77/696) Muhammad ibn al-Hanafiya (82/701) Hasan Basri (102/720)
2. Hasan Ibn Ali (d.50/670)	Kumayl ibn Ziyad Najafi (77/696) Muhammad ibn al-Hanafiya (82/701) Hasan Basri (102/720)
3. Husayn ibn Ali (d.61/680)	Kumayl ibn Ziyad Najafi (77/696) Muhammad ibn Hanafiya (82/701) Hasan Basri (102/720)
4. Ali lbn'l-Husayn (94/712)	Kumayl ibn Ziyad Najafi (77/696) Muhammad ibn al-Hanafiya (82/701)

Hasan Basri (102/720)
Zain'l-Abidin

5. Muhammad al-Baqir (d.114/732)	Hasan Basri (102/720) Malik b. Dinar (137/754)
6. Ja'far al-Sadiq (d.140/757)	Malik b. Dinar (137/754) Habib al-Ajami (156/772) Abu Sulaiman Dawud b. Nusayr al. Ta'i (161/777) Abu Ishaq Ibrahim b. Adham b. Marsus (162/778)
7. Musa al-Kazim (183/799)	Habib al-Ajami (156/772) Dawud al-Tai (161/777) Ibrahim b. Adham (162/778) Abdul Wahid b. Zaid (I 70/786) Ra'bya Basri (185/801) Abu Ali al-Fudayl b. 'Iyad (186/802) Hudhi'a Mar'ashi (I 90/805) Abu Ali Shaqiq b. Ibrahim al-Azdi Balkhi (194/809)
8. Ali al-Raza (202/817)	Abu Ali al-Fudayl b. 'Iyad (186/802) Abu Ali Shaqiq b. Ibrahim al-Azdi Balkhi (194/809) Hubai'ra Basri (200/815) Abu Mahfuz M'aruf Al-Firuz Al-Kharkhi (200/815)
9. Muhammad at-Taqi (221/835)	Al-Sayyida Nafisa (209/824) Sa'id al-Khairwani (211/826) Abu Sulayman Abd'l-Rahman b. Atiyy al-Darani (215/830) Alla'uddin Dainuri (221/835) Bishr b. al-Harith al-Hafi (227 /841)

10. Ali an-Naqi (254/868)	Bishr b. AI-Harith al-Hafi (227 /841) Fatima Naishapuri (235/849) Abu Abd'l-Rahman Hatim b.Ulwan al-Asam (237 /851) Abu Hamid Ahmad b. Khadruya al Balkhi (240/854) Abu Asadullah al-Harith b. Asad al-Mughasibi (245/859) Abul Fayd Dhu'l-Nun b. Ibrahim al-Misri (245/859) Abu Bakr Askar b. AI-Husayn al-Nhsshabi al-Nasafi (245/859) Abul Hasan Sarib. Mughallis al-Saqti (253/867) Fatah al-Sa'ud al-Mulki (257/870) Abu Zakariyya Yahya b. Mu'adh (258/871) Abu Yazid Tayfur b. Isa al-Bistami (261/874)
11. Hasan al-Askari (259/872)	Sari al-Saqti (253/867) Yahya b. Mu'adh (258/871) Abu Yazid al-Bistami (261/874) Abu Hamza As-Sufi (270/883)
12. Lesser Occultation of the 12th Imam (259/872- 1. Othman b. Sa'id, the First Agent of the Hidden Imam (910 ?) 2. Abu Ja'far Muhammad b.	abu Hamza as-Sufi (270/ 883) Abul Qasim al-Mardani (278/ 891) Abu Muhammad Sahl b. Abdullah al-Tustari 283/896 Abu Sa'ad b. Isa Al-Kharraz (286/ 899)

Uthman (305/917), the Second Agent	Abu Ishaq Shami Chisti (291 / 903) Umru Bin Uthman Makki (291/903) Abul Hasan al-Nuri (295/ 907)
3. Abu Qasim ibn Rt1h, the Third Agent (922 ?)	Abul Qasim al-Junayd (297 /909) Amr b. Uthman al-Makki (297/909) Abu Muhammad Rawim (285/898)
4. Abul Hasan Ali Ibn Muhammad Samarri (329/940)	Abu Muhammad Rawim Baghdadi (303/915) Al-Husayn b. Mansur al-Hallaj (310/922)
Greater Occultation of the 12th Imam (329/940-	Abu Muhammad Jariri (311/923) Abu Abdlallah Muhammad b. Ali al-Tirmidhi (320/932) Abu Bakr Muhammad b. Musa al-Wasiti (320/932) Abu Ali Muhammad b. al-Qasim al-Rudhbari (323/934) Abu Bakr b. Dulaf b. Jahdar al-Shibli (334/ 945)

دَائِرَةُ الرَحِيم

أَيْمَن قَوْسِ

أَيْسَر قَوْسِ

الرَحِيمِيَّةُ

الرَحِيم

رَحْمَةٌ وُجُودِيَّةٌ

كُلِّيَاتُ مَرَاتِبِ طَبَقَة مُؤْمِنِين

وَبِهَذَا الاعْتِبَارِ حُكُمُ الأُصُولِ يَسْرِي فِي الفُرُوعِ فَلِكُلّ حَرْفٍ مِن حُرُوفِ البَسْمَلَةِ وَالفَاتِحَةِ وَلِكُلّ سُوَرَة اجمالا و لآياتها وكلماتها وَحُرُوفِهَا تَفْصِيلا دَائِرَةٌ مُقَوَّسَةٌ بِقَوْسَيْنِ وَبَرْزَخٌ جَامِعٌ بَيْنَهُمَا وَذَلِكَ لا يَسَعُ فِي هَذَا المختصر ولا في جميع العوالم كَمَا قَالَ اللّهُ تَعَالَى (قُلْ لَوْ كَانَ البحرُ مِدَادًا لِكَلِمَاتِ رَبِّي لنفد البحرُ قَبْلَ أَن تَنْفَدَ كَلِمَاتُ رَبِّي وَلَوْ جِئْنَا بِمِثْلِهِ مَدَدًا) فَاكْتَفَيْنَا عَلَى مَا رَقَمْنَا و اللّهُ يَقُولُ الحَقَّ وَهُوَ يَهْدِي السبيل وَهُوَ حَسْبُنَا وَنِعْمَ الوَكِيلُ اللّهُمَّ صل على سيدنا محمد أَوَّلِ كُلِّ شَيءٍ وَأَوْسَطِ كل شيءٍ واخر كل شيءٍ كما تحب وترضى وعلى اله وَعِتْرَتِهِ وَاحْفَادِ هِ وأَصْحَابِهِ وَعَشِيرَتِهِ من الأَنْبِيَاءِ والمرسلين والأولياء الصالحين برحمتك يا ارحم الراحمين

فِي غَيْرِهَا وَ اثْبت الاسم فِي القَوْسِ الأَيْمَنِ وَ كُلِّيَّاتِ المَرَاتِبِ فِي الأَيْسَرِ لأَنَ رَحْمَةَ الرَّحْمَنِ وَسِعَتْ كُلَّ شَيْءٍ وَكُلُّ مَنْ وَسِعَتْهُ الرَّحْمَةُ فهو مَرحُومُ وَاثْبِتِ الرَّحْمَةَ فِي البرزخ كما تراهُ

دَائِرَةُ الرَّحْمَنِ

أَيْمَنْ   قَوْسٍ

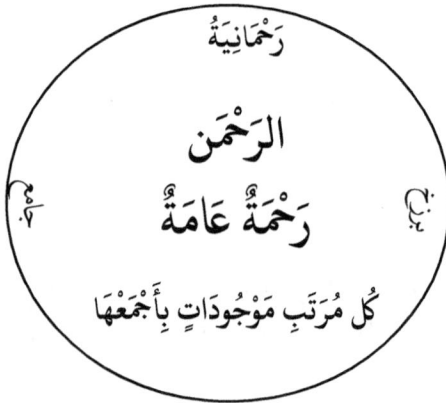

رَحْمَانِيَةٌ

الرَّحْمَن
رَحْمَةٌ عَامَةٌ

كُلُّ مُرَتَبٍ مَوْجُودَاتٍ بِأَجْمَعِهَا

أَيْسَرْ   قَوْسٍ

وَافْعَلُ فِي الرَّحِيمِ مَا فَعَلْتَ فِي الرَّحْمَنِ إِلَّا انَ رَحْمَةَ الرَّحِيمِ رَحْمَةٌ وجُودِيَةٌ مُتَعَلِّقَةٌ بِالْعَمَلِ فَمَرحُومُهَا المُؤْمِنُونَ الَّذِينَ يَعْمَلُونَ الصَّلَحَتِ فَاثْبِت اسمِ الرَّحِيمِ فِي الايمن واسم المؤمِنينَ فِي الايسر والرَّحْمَةِ فِي البرزخ كما تراه

وَالقَابِلة في الايْسَرِ و الحقيقَة المُستعدة لهما في البرْزَخِ كما ترى فَاشْهَدْ هَكَذا

دائِرَةُ اللهِ

قَوْس أَيْمَن

رَبُوبِيّة

صِفَاتٌ فَاعِلَةٌ وُجوبِية مَظاهِرَ الله

مُسْتَعِد حَقِيقَة جَامِعَة الرَّبُوبِيَّةِ و الإنْسَانِيَة

صِفَاتٌ قَابِلَة إِمْكَانِيّة مَظاهِرَ الله

عَبُودِيّة

قَوْس أَيْسَر

وَ أَمَّا الرَّحْمَنُ فَهُوَ اسمٌ لَلْحَقِ بِاعْتِبَارِ اِنْبِسَاطِ الوُجُودِ عَلَى الأَعْيَانِ وَ الرَّحِيمُ اسمٌ لَهُ بِاعْتِبَارِ اختِصاصِه مِنْ كُلِّ عَيْنٍ بِحِصَةٍ من حصص الوُجُودِ فَالْحَقّ بِنَفْسِهِ الرَّحمةُ الإمْتِنانِيّةُ العَامَّةُ المخصوصة بِالرَّحْمَنِ والوُجُودِيّة الخاصة المتصلة بالرَّحِيمِ يَزِيدُ ظهور المَرْحُومِ لِيَظْهَرَ بِه سِرُّ رَحْمَةِ الرَّحْمَانِيَّةِ وَبِاعْمَالِ المرحومِينَ عند اعْطَاء جَزَائِهُمْ رَحِميّة فَوقَعَتْ نِسْبَةُ الرَّحْمَةِ بَيْنَ المنتَسِبِينَ وَهُوَ الرَّحْمَنُ وَالرَّحِيمُ والمرحومُ فَافْهُمْ فَإِذَا فَهِمْتَ فَارسم دائرة لإسْمِ الرحمن فافعل فيها مَا فَعَلْتَ

عليها دَائِرَةً فَارْسِمْهَا وَاجْعَلْهَا قَابَ قَوْسَيْنِ بِخَطٍّ مَارٍ فِي وَسَطِهَا
فَثَبِّتِ الْبَسَمَ فِي الْقَوْسِ الْأَيْمَنِ وَالرَّحْمنِ الرَّحِيمِ فِي الْقَوِسِ الْأَيْسَرِ وَ
اللّهُ فِي الْبَرْزَخِ لِانه اسم لِلذَّاتِ الْمَوْصُوفَةِ بِجميعِ الْأَسْمَاءِ وَالصِّفَاتِ
فَهُوَ بَرْزَخٌ مِنْ حَيْثُ جَمْعِيَّتِهِ لِلْقِسْمَيْنِ وَهِيَ هذا

هَذِهِ دَائِرَةُ أُمُّ الْأُمِّ يَعْنِي بَسْمَلَةٌ

قَوْسٌ أَيْمَنْ

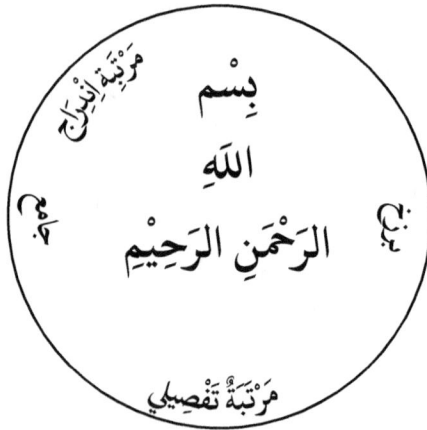

قَوْسٌ أَيْسَرْ

واعلَمْ أَنَّ الْبَسَمَلَةَ مُشْتَمَلَةٌ عَلَى ثَلَثَةِ اسماء وهي الله والرَّحْمنُ
وَالرَّحِيمُ وَ بَرْزَخٌ جامع فاما الله فهو مشتمل على الْجميع الاسماء
والصَّفَاتِ الْفَاعِلَةِ وَالْقَابِلَةِ والحقيقةِ الْمُسْتَعِدَةِ لِلْفَاعِلَةِ وَالْقَابِلَةِ
فارسم فيها دَائِرَةً أُخْرَى كَمَا قُلْتُ وَ اثْبِتِ الْفَاعِلَةَ فِي الْأَيْمَنِ

فَاهْلُ السَّعَادَةِ والهداية وَهُمْ أَصْحَابُ الْيَمِينِ مَظْهَرُ الجمالِ وَ
أَهْلِ الشَّقَاوَةِ وَالضَّلَةِ وَهُمْ أَصْحَابُ الشمَالِ مَظْهَرُ الْجَلَالِ وَلَا
بُدَّ أَنْ يَكُونَ لَهُمَا مَقَامَانِ لِيَظْهَرَ فِيهِمَا أَحْكَامُهُمَا وَ أَخْلَاقُهُمَا وَ
أَعْمَالُهُمَا وَ هُمَا الْجَنَّةُ وَالنَّارُ وَجَمِيعُ ذَلِكَ مندرج في القِسْمِ الَّذِي
يَتَعَلَّقَ الْعَبْدَ واما القِسْمُ المتعلق بِالْحَقِّ وَالْعَبْدِ مَعًا الَّذِي سُمّى
بِالْحَقِيقَةِ الْكُلِّيَّةِ الانسانيَّةِ فَهُوَ مَرْتَبَةُ أَهْلِ الْكَمَالِ وَمَقَامُ الْمُطلع
وَ مُنَزِلُ الْأَشْرَافِ على الْأَطْرَافِ وَمَوْقِفُ الْأَعْرَافِ قال الله تَعَالَى
وَعَلَى الْأَعْرَافِ رِجَال يعرفون كلّاً بِسِيمَاهُمْ لانهم مُحِيطُونَ على الكل
وَلَهُمُ الْكَمَالُ المتعلق بالذات والجلال والجمالِ مُنْدَرَجَان في الْكَمَالِ
وَارْبَابُ هَذَا الْمَوْقِفِ الْعَارِفُونَ الْمُوَحِّدُونَ وَإِذَا تقرر هذا فَاعْلَمْ
ان في هذا البَرْزَخِ يَتَصِفُ الحَقُّ تَعَالَى بصفاتِ الْعَبْدِ مِنَ الضحْكِ
وَالْبُكَاءِ والبَشَاشَةِ وَالْفَرْح وَالْمَكْرُ والاستهزاء والمَرض وَالْجُوعِ
وَالْعَطَشِ وَمَا اشْبَهَ ذلك وَالْعَبْدُ يَتَصِفُ بِصَفَاتِ الْحَقِّ تَعَالَى من
الحيوة وَالْعِلْمِ وَالْأَرَادَةِ وَالْقُدْرَةِ والسمع والبصَر والكلام والاحياء
والاماتة وَالانْبِسَاطِ وَالانْقِبَاضِ والتَّصَرُّفِ في الْأَكْوَانِ وَغَيْر ذَلِكَ
فَهَذَا البرْزَخُ هُوَ مَرْتَبَةُ التَّنَزُّل الرَّبَّانِي لِيَتَصِفَ الرَّبُّ فيها بِالصَّفَاتِ
العبدانيَّةِ وَمَرْتَبَةُ ارْتِفَاع الْعَبْدِ لِيَتَصِفَ الْعَبْدُ فِيهَا بِالصَّفَاتِ
الرَّبَّانِيَّةِ فَهِيَ الْعَمَى المذكور في الحديثِ الْمَشْهُورِ وَلَوْلَا اَنِّي أَخَافُ
عن التطويل وَالْأَعْرَاضِ عَنِ التَّوْحِيدِ لَذَكرت في هذِهِ المَرْتَبَةِ
الْعَمَائِيَّةِ اسرارها فاخَذْتُ لِذَلِكَ عِنَانَ القَلَم وَاكْتَفَيْتُ بِمَا يَلِيقُ
بهذا المختصر فَثَبَتَ عَلَى مَا قَرَرْنَا انَّ فَاتِحَة الكِتَابِ جَامِعَة لِجَميع
المَرَاتِب و الْعَوَالِم التي هِيَ الْكِتَابُ وَجَميعُ المَرَاتِب و الْعَوَالِم فِيهَا
مُنْدَرَجَةٌ ولذلِكَ سُمِّيَتْ بِأُم الْكِتَابِ - و اما البسمَلَةُ المَوسُومَةُ بِأُم
الْأُمِ فهى ايضا عَلَى قِسْمَيْنِ قِسْم مِنْهَا مَا يَتَعَلَّقُ بالذات وَهُوَ الْبِسْمُ
وَقِسْم يَتَعَلَّقُ بالصفاتِ وَهُوَ الرَّحْمَنُ الرَّحِيمُ وَمَا بينهما فَهُوَ جَامِعٌ
لِلْقِسْمَيْنِ وَمُقَابِلِهِمَا وَهِيَ فِيهِ جَمْعُ وَهُوَ اللّهُ وَهُوَ اللّهُ وَإِنْ شِئْتَ أَنْ ترسم

قِسْمًا للحق وقِسْمًا للعبدِ وَقِسْمًا جَامِعا لهُمَا وَهِيَ هَذِهِ

إلَهِي — قَوْس

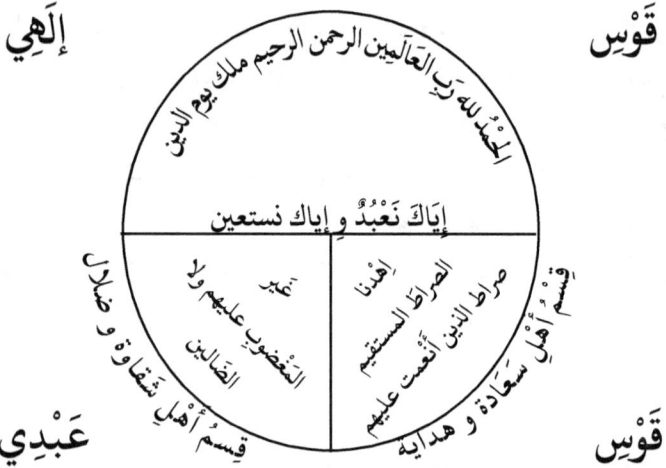

عَبْدِي — قَوْس

واعلم ان هذه الدَّائِرَةُ الكلية مشتملة على جَمِيع المَوْجُودَاتِ جَبَرُوتِهَا وَمَلَكُوتِهَا وَبَرْزَخٍ جَامِعٍ وَمُلْكِهَا فَمَا يتعلق بِالحَقِّ مِنها يُسمى بِالجَبَرُوتِ وما يتعلق بِالعَبْدِ يَنْقَسِمُ قِسْمين قِسْم سُمى بِالمَلَكُوت وَ قِسْم سُمّى بِالمُلْكِ فَإِن لِلْعَبْدِ رُوَحًا وَجَسْما رُوْحه شامِل لِلْمَلَكُوتِ وَجِسْمُهُ شامِل لِلْمُلْكِ وَمَا يَتَعَلَّقُ بِالحَقِّ وَالْعَبْدِ مَعًا سُمى بِالحَقِيقَةِ الكلية الانسانِيَةِ وَالْقِسْمُ الَّذِي يَتَعَلَّقُ بِالعَبْدِ كَمَا قُسَمَ قِسْمَيْنِ وَسُمِّي كُلُّ قسم باسم كَذلِكَ خُصِصَ قِسْمُ بِأهل السَعَادَةِ وَالهَدَايَةِ وَهُوَ مِنْ اَهْدِنَا الصِراط المُسْتَقِيمَ إِلَى اَنْعَمْتَ عَلَيْهِمْ وقسم بِأَهلِ الشَّقَاوَةِ وَالضَلَّةِ وَهُوَ مِنْ غَيْرِ الْمَغْضُوبِ عَلَيْهِمْ إِلَى ولا الضَالِينَ وَذلِكَ لِأَنَ عَالَم الجبروت جَامِعُ لِلْجَلَالِ وَالجَمَالِ ولابد أن يَكُونَ لَهُمَا مَظَهَرَانِ ليظهر بِهِمَا احْكَامُهُمَا

وَلَا شَكَّ أَنَّ الْعَرْشَ كَانَ مُنْدَرِجاً فِي الْعَقْلِ الَّذِي هُوَ الْقَلَمُ وَالْفَاتِحَةَ إِشَارَةً إِلَى الْكِتَابِ الْجَامِعِ وَهُوَ الاِنْسَانُ وَلَا شَكَّ أَنَّ الْإِنْسَانَ قبلَ ظُهُورِهِ كَانَ مُنْدَرِجا فِي جَمِيعِ الْمَرَاتِبِ كَانْدِرَاجِ الْكُلِّ فِيهِ بَعْدَ ظهوره وانبساط التُّقْطة فِي ذَاتِهَا إِشَارَةً إِلى الكِتَابِ الْمُبِينِ الأَوَّلِ وَانْبِسَاطُ الْبَاءِ بالسين اشَارَةٌ إِلَى الكِتَابِ الْمُبِينِ الثَّانِي وَتَفْصِيلُ حُرُوفِ الْبَسْمَلَةِ وَتَدَاخُلُ بعضها فِي البعض إِشَارَةٌ إِلَى الكِتَابِ الْمُبِينِ الثَّالِثِ وَتَكْرَارُ مَا فِي الْبَسْمَلَةِ فِي الْفَاتِحَةِ وَتَضَاهِي بَعْضُهَا لِلْبَعْضِ إشارة إِلَى الكتاب المبين الرابع وجَمِيعُ الْقُرَانِ مِنَ الفَاتِحَةِ إِشَارَةٌ إِلَى مَرَاتِبِ الْعَالَمِ وَ اجزَائِهَا فَا فْهَمْ وَ إِذَا تَقَرَّرَ هذا فَاعْلَمْ ان الفاتحة تَنْقَسِمُ عَلَى ثَلَثَةِ اقسام قسم متعلق بالحَقِّ وَقِسم مُتَعَلِّقَ بالخلق وَقِسْمُ جَامِعُ بَيْنَهُمَا كَمَا روى ابو هُرَيْرَةَ رض عَنِ النَّبِيِّ صَلَّى اللهُ عَلَيْهِ وسلم انه قَالَ (مَنْ صَلَّى صَلوةً لَمْ يَقْرَأْ فِيهَا أُمَّ الْكِتَابِ فَهِيَ خَدَاجُ ثَلَثًا أى غَيْرُ تَمَام فقِيلَ لِأَبِي هُرَيْرَةَ رض إِنَّا نَكُونَ وَرَاءَ الامام قال اقراءَهَا فِي نَفْسِكَ فَإِنِّي سَمِعْتُ رَسُولَ اللهِ صَلَّى اللهُ عَلَيْهِ وَسَلَّمَ يَقُولُ قَالَ اللهُ تَعَالَى قَسَمْتُ الصَّلوة بَيْنِي وَبَيْنَ عَبْدِى نِصْفَيْنِ وَ لِعَبْدِي مَا سَأَلَ فَإِذَا قَالَ الْعَبْدُ الْحَمْدُ لِلَّهِ رب العلمين قَالَ اللهُ تَعَالَى حَمَدَنِي عَبْدِي وَإِذَا قَالَ الرَّحْمَنِ الرَّحِيمِ قَالَ اللهُ تعالى أَثْنَى عَلَى عَبْدِي و إِذا قال مَالِكِ يَوْمِ الدِّينِ قَالَ اَللهُ تَعَالَى مَجَدَنِي عَبْدِي و إِذا قَالَ الْعَبْدُ إِيَّاكَ نَعْبُدُ وَإِيَّاكَ نَسْتَعِينُ قَالَ الله تعالى هَذَا بَيْنِي وَبَيْنَ عَبْدِي وَلِعَبْدِي مَا سَأَلَ وَ إِذَا قَالَ اهِدِنَا الصِّرَاطَ الْمُسْتَقِيمَ صِرَاطَ الَّذِينَ أَنْعَمْتَ عَلَيْهِمْ غَيْرِ الْمَغْضُوبِ عَلَيْهِمْ وَلَا الضَّالِّينَ – قَالَ الله تعالى هَذَا بَيْنِي وَبَيْنَ عَبْدِي وَلِعَبْدِي مَا سَأَلَ فَالْفَاتِحَة من أولها إلى مُلِكِ يَوْمِ الدِّينِ متعلق بالحَقِّ الصَّرْفِ وَإِيَّاكَ نَعْبُدُ وَايَّاكَ نَسْتَعِينُ مُتَعَلَّقٌ بِالْحَقِّ وَالْعَبْدِ و من اهدِنَا الصِّرَاطَ الْمُسْتَقِيمَ إِلَى آخِرِ الْفَاتِحَة متعلق بالعَبْدِ الصَّرْفِ وَلِتَحْقِيق هذه الاقسام الثلاثة رسمنَا دَائِرَةً وَقَسَمْنَاهَا بِقِسْمَيْنِ بسبب خَطٍّ مَارٍّ بَيْنَهُمَا وَجَعَلْنَهَا

عِلْمُ الكِتَابِ (وَلَا رَطب) اى عالَمُ الْمُلْكِ (وَلَا يَابِسٍ) وَهُوَ عَالَم
الْمَلَكُوتِ وَلَا أَعْلَى مِنْهُ (الا فِي كِتَاب مبين) وَهُوَ انت وَأَمَّا الْكِتَابُ
الذى أُنْزِلَ عَلَى الانْسَانِ الْكَامِلِ فَهُوَ بَيَانُ المراتب لكلية الْجُمَلِيَّةِ
والجزئية التفصيلية الإنْسَانِيَّةِ فَهُوَ بَيَانُ الْكِتَابِ وَالْإِنْسَانُ الكامل
مرتبة وَحْدَتِهِ وَجَمْعِيَّتِهِ وَقَدْ فَضَلَ مَرَاتِبَ تَفْصِيلِهِ لِأَنَّهُ بَيْنَ الْفَرْقَ
بين مَقَامَاتِهِ وَمَرَاتِبِهِ وَاَطْوَارِهِ وَاَدْوَارِهِ وَذَا تِهِ وَصِفَاتِهِ وَافْعَالِهِ لانه
يحكى عَنِ الذات والأَسْمَاءِ وَالصَّفَاتِ وَالأَفْعَالِ وعن العوالم وَاهْلِهَا
وَمَرَاتِب العوالم و أَهْلِهَا وَ اَحْوَالِ الْعَوَالِمِ وَاهْلِهَا فِي كُلِّ موطن مِنَ
الْمَوَاطِينِ وَعَنِ اقْتِضَاء أَهْلِهَا إِجْمَالاً وَ تَفْصِيلاً وَهَذِه تَفَاصِيلُ
مَرَاتِبِ الإنْسَانِ وَهُوَ مَجْمُوعَ جَمِيعِهَا فَثَبَتَ أَنَّ هذا الكتاب مُعَرِّفُ
الإِنْسَانِ وَمُبَيِّنُ مَرَاتِبِهِ الكلية والجزئيّة وَإِذَا تَقَرَّر هذا فاعلم ان
هذا الكِتَابِ لَمُنَزَّلَ عَلَى الإِنْسَانِ الكامِلِ فَاتِحَةَ مُسَمَى بِأَمِّ الْكِتَابِ
وَ جَمِيعُ مَا فِي الْكِتَابِ مُفَصَّلَ فِيهَا مُجْمَل وَمَا فِيهَا مُجْمَل فَهُوَ فِي
الْكِتَابِ مُفَصَّل والفاتحة في الْبَسْمَلَةِ وَالبَسْمَلَةُ في الْبَاءِ والْبَاء في
النُّقْطَةِ مَنْدَرَجَةً فَهِي أَمُّ الكِتاب وجَميعُ الكِتَابِ كَائِنَ فِيهِ الْحُرُوف
المقطعات وَالْمُتَّصِلاتُ وَالأَلفاظ و الكلمات والسُّورُ والايَات
والكتاب عبارة عن انْبِسَاطِهَا وَتَعَينها بِجَمِيعِهَا واندراجُ الكُل فِيهَا
عِبَارَةٌ عَنْ عَدَم انبِسَاطِهَا إِذْ مَا ثَمَّهَ شَيْء غَيْرُهَا فَمَنْ عَرَفَ ما قُلْنَا
عَرَفَ مَعْنى قَوْلِهِ تَعَالَى (ألم تَرَ إلى رَبَّكَ كيف مَدَ الظَّلَ وَلَوْ شَاء
لَجَعَلَهُ سَاكِنًا)، فَمَدَ الظَّل عِبَارَة عن انبساط النقطة الوُجوديّة و
تَعَينها بتَعَيّنَاتِ الحُرُوف الالَهيّةِ وَ الكونيّة وَالسُّكُونُ عِبَارَةٌ عَنْ
عَدَمِ انبساط النُّقْطَةِ الوُجُودِيَّةِ وَتَعَيّنها بتعيناتِ الحُرُوف الالهية
والكونية و عدم بقائِهَا عَلَى بَسَاطتها الْمُنَبَّهَة عليها في قوله تعالى
(كنتُ كنزاً) فَهَذِه النُّقْطَةُ البَائيَّةُ إِشَارَة إِلَى النُّقْطَةِ الوجوديّة وَبَاء
الْبَسْمَلَةِ إِشَارَةٌ إِلَى أم الكِتَابِ الثَّانِي وَهُوَ الْقَلَمُ وَلا رَيْبَ أنَّهُ كَانَ
فِيهِ مُنْدَرَجًا وَالْبَسْمَلَةُ إشارة إلى أم الْكِتَابِ الثَّالِثِ وَهُوَ العرش

قَالَ ابي امير الْمُؤمنينَ عَلَى بن أَبي طَالِبٍ كرم الله وجهه شعر

دَآءكَ فِيكَ وَمَا تشعر

دَواءكَ مِنْكَ وَمَا تُبْصِرُ

وَتَزْعَمُ أَنَّكَ جُرمٌ صَغِيرُ

وَفِيكَ انطوى العالم الاكبر

وانت الكتاب المبين الذي

بِاحْرُفِه يَظْهَرُ المضمر

فَلَا حَاجَةً لَكَ مِن خارج

وفكرك فِيكَ وَمَا تَفكر

أما تَسمع كَيْفَ يَقُولُ الحَقُّ عَزَّوَجَلَ اقرأ كتبكَ كَفَى بِنَفْسِكَ الْيَوْمَ عَلَيْكَ حسيبا) فمن قرأ هذا الكِتَابَ فَقَدْ علم مَا كَانَ وَمَا هُوَ كَائِن وَمَا هُوَ يَكُونُ فان لم تقرأ بتمامِه فَاقْرَأْ مَا تَسَيَر مِنْهُ ألا ترى كيفَ يَقُولُ الحَقُّ سُبْحَانَه (سنريهم ايتنا في الافاق وَفي أَنفُسِهِمْ حَتَّى يَتبين لهمْ أَنَّهُ الْحَقُّ) وَكَيْفَ يَقُولُ سُبْحَانَهُ وتعالى (وفي أَنفسكم أفلا تبصرون) وكيف يقول سبحانه وتعالى (آلم ذلك الكتاب لا ريب فيه) الألفُ يُشَارُ به الى الأحدية الذاتية أي الحَقِّ مِنْ حَيْثُ هُوَ اوَلُ الاشياء في أزَلَ الأزَال – وَاللَّامُ يُشَارُ بِه إلى الوجود المُنْبَسِطِ عَلَى الأَعْيَان فإن اللامَ لَهُ قَائِمَةٌ وَهي الالفُ وَلَهُ ذيل وَهِي دَائِرَةُ النُّونِ – وَالنُّونُ عِبَارَةُ عن دائرة الكون فَاتِصَالُ القائمة بالذيل دَلِيلُ انبساطِ الْوُجُودِ عَلَى الكَوْنِ الجامع، والميم يشارُ بِه إلَى الكون الجامع وهو الانسانُ الْكَامِلُ فَالْحَقُّ وَالْعَالَمُ والإنسانُ الْكَامِل كِتَابٌ لَا رَيْبَ فيه ولذلك قال الله تعالى (قل كفى بالله شهيدًا بيني وَبَينَكُمْ وَمَنْ عِنْدَه علم الكِتَابُ) فَهَذا يا وَلَدِى هُوَ الكِتَابُ وعلم الكتاب وانت الكِتَابُ كَمَا قلتُ وَ عِلْمُكَ بِكَ

الاتحاد يحصلُ مِنَ الْوُجُودَين وكذا الحلولُ وَالصَّيرُورَةُ وَمَا ثَمَ إلا
وجُودُ وَاحِد و الاشياء مَوْجُودَةٌ بِهِ مَعْدُومَةٌ بِنَفْسِهَا فَكَيفَ يتحدُ
مَنْ هُوَ مَوْجُودٌ بِهِ وَمَعْدُومٌ بِنَفْسِهِ ولو تسمَعُ الاتحادِ مِنْ أَهْلِ اللَّهِ أَوْ
تَجِدُ في مصنفاتِهِمْ فَلَا تَفْهُمْ مَا فَهِمْتَ مِن الاتحادِ الذِي قُلْنَا فِيهِ إنَّهُ
يَحْصُلُ مِنَ الْوُجُودَين إذْ لَيسَ مُرَادُهُمْ بِالاتحادِ الا شهودُ الْوُجُودِ
الحَقِّ الْوَاحِدِ الْمُطلقِ الَّذِي الكُلِّ بِهِ مَوْجُودٌ فيتحد بِهِ الكلِّ من حيث
كونِ كلِّ شَى مَوْجُودَا بِهِ وَمَعْدُمَّا في نَفْسِهِ لَا مِنْ حَيْثُ أَنَّ لَهُ وجودًا
خاصًّا اتحَدَ بِهِ الكُلِّ فَإنَّهُ مُحَال ولهذا الوُجُودِ الْوَاحِدِ ظُهُورُ وَ هُوَ
الْعَالَمُ وبُطونَ وَهُوَ الْأَسْمَاء وَبَرْزَحُ جَامِعُ فاصل بينهما لِيَتميز به
الظهور عن البطون وَهُوَ الْإنْسَانُ الكَامِلُ فَالظهور مرآة الظهور و
البطونَ مِرآة البطون و ما كان بينَهُمَا فَهُوَ مِرآة جَمْعًا وَ تَفصيلًا وإذا
تَقَرَرَ هُذَا فَلْيَرْجِعُ إلى ماكنا بسبيله فَتَقُولُ كَمَا آنَ بَيْنَ ذَاتِ الحَقِّ
ذَاتِ الانسانِ الكَامِل وَعِلْمَ الْحَقِّ وَعِلم مضاهاةٌ وَأَنَّ كُلَّ مَا فيهَا
مُجْمَل فهو فيها مجمل وكلِّ مَا فيهِ مُفَصَّل فَهُوَفيهِ مفصل كَذَلِكَ بَيْنَ
القَلَمِ وَرُوحِ الْإنْسَانِ واللوح وقلب الْإنْسَانِ وَ العرش وجسم
الانسان والكُرسي وَنَفَسَ الانسان مضاهاةً وَكُلِّ وَاحِدٍ مِنْهَا مِرآة
لِمَا يضاهيه فَكُلِّ مَا في القَلَمِ مجمل فهو في روحه مجمل و كل ما في
اللوح مُفَصَّل فَهُوَ في قلبه مُفَصَّل وَكُلِّ مَا في العَرْشِ مُجْمَل فهو في
جسمه مُجْمَل وَكل مَا في الكرسي مُفَصل فهو في نَفْسِهِ مُفَصَّل
فَالْإنْسَانُ كِتَابٌ جامع لِجَميع الكتب الالهية والكونية كما قُلْنَا في
حَقِّ الْحَقِّ إنَّ عِلْمَهُ بِذَاتِهِ مُسْتَلْزِمٌ لِعِلمِهِ بِجَميعِ الْأَشْيَاء وَإنَّهُ يعلم
جميع الاشياء مِنْ عِلْمِهِ بِذَاتِهِ كذلك نَقُولُ في حَقِّ الْإنْسَانِ
الكَامِل ان عِلْمَهُ بِذَاتِهِ مُستلزم لِعَلمهِ بِجَميعِ الأشياء وَإنَّهُ
يَعْلَمُ جَميعَ الْأَشْيَاء من علمه بذاتِهِ لأنه هُوَ جَميعُ الاشياء إجمالا
وتفصيلًا فَمَنْ عَرَفَ نَفْسَهُ عرف ربَّه وَعَرَفَ جَميعَ الْأَشْيَاء
ففكركَ يَا وَلدِى فِيكَ يَكْفِيكَ فليس شىء خَارِجًا مِنْكَ كَمَا

الجزئي والتَّفصيلي فَهُوَ في الكرسي ثابِتٌ على الوجه الجزئي والتَّفصيلي
فَالقَلَمُ المكنى بالعقل نموذج الذاتِ ومراتها وَمَظْهَرُها وَمَنَصَّتُها
وَمُجلاها واللوحُ المُسَمَّى بِالنَّفسِ نموذج القَلَمِ وَمرآتُه ومظهرُه
وَمَنَصَّتُه وَمُجلاه وَالعَرش نموذج القَلَمِ و مِراتُه و مظهره وَمَنَصَّتُه
ومجلاه والكرسي نموذج اللوحو مرآته وَمَظْهَرُهُ وَمَنَصَّتُهُ وَمُجلاه
فالعقلُ نُسخةُ الذَّاتِ وَاللَّوْحُ نُسخةُ العِلمِ والعرش نسخة القلم
والكرسى نسخة اللوح واما الإنْسَانُ العَامِلُ فَهُوَ نُسخةٌ جامعة
لِجميع النسخ وَهُوَ المُسْتَخْرَجُ و المستنبط مِنَ الْكُلِّ وَهُوَ الْجَامِعُ
بَيْنَ الْحقائق الالهية والكونية فكما ان ذات الحق كِتَابٌ جُملي وَأمٌ
جَامعٌ لِجميع الكتاب قَبْلَ تَفصيلِهَا وَعِلمُهُ تَعَالَى بِنَفسِه كِتَابٌ
مُبِينٌ تَفصيلي مُفَصَّل مبين فِيه مَا كَانَ في الذَّاتِ مُضمَراً كَذلكَ
الإنسانُ الْكَامِلُ كِتَابٌ جُملي وَأمٌ جَامعُ الجميع الكتب بَعْدَ تَفصيلِها
و علم بِنَفْسِه كِتَابٌ مُبَيِّنٌ تَفصيلي مُفَصَّلٌ مُبيِّنٌ فِيه مَا كان
فيالإنسان الْكَامِل مُجْمَلَا فعلمُ الإنْسَان الكامل بِذَاتِه مِراةٌ لِذَاتِه
وَذَاتُه ظَاهِرَةٌ فِيه وَمَمَيَّزَةٌ بِه كَمَا أنَّ عِلمَ الْحَقَّ بِذَاتِه مراة بذاتِه
وَذَاتُه ظَاهِرَةٌ فِيه مُتَعَيِّنَةٌ به فبَيْنَ ذَاتِ الْحَقَّ سُبْحَانَهُ وَذَاتِ الإنْسَانِ
الْكَامِل مُضَاهَاةً مِن جهةِ الكليّةِ والإجْمَالِ وَكُونُ الأَشْيَاء فِيها عَلَى
الوَجْهِ الْكُلِّ والإجْمَالي وَبَيْنَ عِلمِ الْحَقَّ وَعِلمِ الإنْسَانِ الكَامِل
مُضَاهَاةً مِنْ حَيْثُ مَظْهَرِيَّتَهُ لِتَفصيلِ ما أجمل فَالْإنْسَانُ الْكَامِلُ
مِراةٌ تَامَّةٌ لِلذاتِ بِسَبَبِ هَذِه المُضَاهَاةِ والذات متجليةٍ عَلَيْه عَلَى
الوجه الكلي والجملي وَعِلمُ الإنْسَان الْكَامِل مِرآة لِعِلمِ الْحَقَّ و علم
الْحَقَّ مُتَجَلٍّ عَلَيْهِ وَظَاهِرٌ بِه فَمَا في الذاتِ مُنْدَرِجٌ عَلَى الوَجْهِ الكُلِّي
و الاجمالي فهو في الإنْسان الكامل مُندرج على ذلكَ الوَجْهِ وَمَا فِي
عِلمِ الْحَقَّ ظَاهِرٌ عَلى الوجهِ الْجُزْئي وَالتَّفصيلي فَهُوَ فِي علم الإنسانِ
الكَامِل ظَاهِرُ عَلَى الوَجْهِ الجزئي وَالتَّفصيلي بَل علمُهُ عِلمه و ذاته
ذاته بلا اتحادٍ مَعَهُ وَلَا حُلُولٍ فِيهِ وَلَا صَيْرُورَته هُوَ لانها محال لان

أم الكِتَابِ وَالذَّاتُ ظَاهِرٌ فِيهَا لأَنَّ الْعِلْمَ هُوَ اوَّلُ مَا تَعَيَّنَ بِهِ الذات
فالذاتُ هِيَ أُمُّ الْكِتَابِ مِنَ الحقائِقِ الالهِيَّةِ وَالْعِلْمُ هُوَ الْكِتَابُ
المبِين مِنَ الْحَقَائِقِ الالهِيَّةِ كَمَا أَنَّ القَلَمَ هُوَ أُمُّ الْكِتَابِ مِنَ الْحَقَائِقِ
الكونية واللوح المحفوظ هُوَ الْكِتَابُ الْمُبِينُ مِنَ الْحَقَائِقِ الْكَوْنِيَةِ
فَبَيْنَ الذَّاتِ وَالْقَلَمِ مُضَاهاة مِنْ جِهةِ الاجمال وَالكُلِّيَّةِ وَكَوْنِ الاشياء
فيهما عَلَى وَجْهِ الْكُلِّ وَكَذَلِكَ بَيْنَ اللوح وَالعِلْمِ مُشَابَهَةٌ مِّنْ جِهةِ
التَّفْصِيلِ وَظُهورِ الأَشْيَاءِ فيهِمَا عَلَى الوجهِ الجُزْئِي فَالْقَلَمُ مِنْ هَذَ
الْوَجْهِ في مَرْتَبَةِ الكَوْنِيَّةِ مِرآةُ الذاتِ فَمَا في الذاتِ مُنْدَرَج عَلَى وَجْهِ
الكُلِّ وَ الإجْمَالِي فَهُوَ في القَلَمِ مُودَع عَلَى الْوَجْهِ الكلِّ والاجْمَالِي
وَاللَّوْح المحفُوظُ ايضا من هذا الوجهِ في المرتبة الكونية مرآة الْعِلْمِ
فَمَا في العِلْمِ عَلَى الْوَجْهِ الجُزْئِي وَالتَّفْصِيل فَهُوَ في التَّوْجِ ظَاهِرٌ عَلَى
الْوَجْهِ الجزئِي وَالتَّفْصِيلِي فهو في اللوح ظاهر على الوجهِ الجزئِي وَ
التفصيلي فَكَمَا عَلِمْتَ آنَ العَالَمَ الأَمْرِ كِتَابًا مُجْمَلاً مُلَقَّبًا بِأُمِّ
الْكِتَابِ وكِتابًا مفصلًا موسُومًا بِالْكِتَابِ المُبِين وَالْكِتَابُ الْمُجْمَلُ
هُوَ العَقْلُ والكتاب المبين هُوَ اللوح المحفوظ فاعلم كذلِكَ آنَ
لِعَالَمِ الْمُلْكِ كِتَابًا مُجملا هُوَ الْعَرْشُ وَكِتَابَا مُفَصَّلا هُوَ الكرسي
فَاعْتِبَارِ انْدِرَاج مَا يُرِيدُ ان يفصلَ في الْكُرْسِي مَا كَانَ في الْعَرْشِ
مُجملا يقال له أُمُّ الْكِتَابِ وَباعْتِبَارِ تَفْصيلِ مَا كَانَ في الْعَرْشِ مُجملاً
في الكرسي يُقَال لَهُ الْكِتَابُ المُبِينُ فَبَيْنَ الْعَرْشِ وَ القلم مُضَاهَاةٌ
مِّنْ جِهَةِ الإجْمَالِ وكون الأشْيَاءِ فيهما عَلَى الْوَجْهِ الكلِّ أو كذلِكَ
بين الكرسي واللوح مناسبة من جهة مَظْهَرِيَّتِهِما وَمِنْ جِهةِ تَقْسِيمِ
امر واحِدٍ فِيهِمَا بِالْقِسْمَيْنِ وَمِنْ جِهةِ ظُهورِ الأَشْيَاء فِيهِمَا عَلَى
الْوَجْهِ الجُزْئِي وَالتَّفْصِيلي فَالْعَرْش مِنْ هَذَا الْوَجْهِ في المرتبة الحسية
مرآة القلم فما في القَلَمِ مُنْدَرَج عَلَى الْوَجْهِ الكلِّ و الاجْمَالِي فَهُوَ في
الْعَرْشِ مُنْدَرَج كذلك وَالكُرْسِيُّ أَيْضًا مِنْ هَذَا الْوَجْهِ في المرتبة
الحسية مرآة اللوح المحفوظ فما في اللوح المحفوظ ثَابِت عَلَى الْوَجْهِ

في ملتمس زين العابدين وَاسئلُ العون من موجدِ الكُونِ فإنهُ المستعانُ وَعَلَيْهِ التَّكلَانُ اعْلَمْ أَيها الوَلَدُ المُؤَيَّدُ انَ الْعَالَمَ عَالَمَان عالم الأمرِ وَعَالَمُ الْخَلقِ وكل وَاحِدٍ مِنْهُمَا كِتَابٌ مِّنْ كُتُبُ اللهِ وَلِكل فاتحة - وَجَمِيعَ مَا في الْكِتَابِ مُفَصل في الفاتحة مُجْمَلُ - فَباعْتِبَارِ اجمال ما فصل في الكتاب فيها سُميت بأم الكِتَابِ وَباعْتَبَارِ تَفْصِيلِ مَا أجمل فيها فيما يلي مرتبتهما سميت مرتبة التَّفْصِيلِ بِالكِتَابِ المُبين - وكل مَوْجُودٍ حَرف بِاعْتِبَارٍ وَكَلِمَةُ باعتبار ومفرَدُ وَمُقَطَعُ بِاعْتِبَارِو ألفاظ مركبة باعْتِبَارِ وَ سُورَةٌ بِاعْتِبَارٍ لأن إذا نظرنا في ذاتِ كل مَوْجُودٍ مِنْ غَيْرِ انْ نَنْظُرَ في وُجُوهِهَا وَخَوَاصِهَا وعوارضها ولوازمها مُجردَةً عَن الكُل فباعتبار تجردها عَن الكل سميناها حَرْفًا وَإذَا نَظَرنا إلى وُجُوهِهَا وَ خواصها وَعَوارِضِهَا وَلَوَازمِهَا وَ أضفناهَا إِلَيْهَا فَباعْتِبَارِها اضافة الكل اليها سميناهَا كلمَةً وَ بِاعْتِبَارِتجرد كُل مَوْجُودٍ عَن الْمُضَافَاتِ وَالْمَنْسُوبَاتِ وتمييز بعضها عَن بَعْضٍ سُمِيَتْ حُروفا مقَطَعَةً مَفَرَدَةً وَبِاعْتِبَارِ عَدَم تجردها عن المضافاتِ والمَنسُوبَاتِ وَعَدَم تمييز بعضها عَنْ بَعْضٍ بَل تداخل بعضها في البعض سُميت الفاظا مرَكَّبَةً و باعْتِبَارِ تَمييز كِلِمَاتِ الْمُرَكَّبِ بعضها عن بَعْضٍ ووقوع كل موجود في مرتبة سميت سُورَةً - فَإِذَا فهمت هذا فاعلم ايضا ان الْحق مبدء الكُل وَمَعَادُه وَ وَالِيهِ يُرْجَعُ الأَمْرُ كله وَإِلَى الله عاقِبَةُ الأُمُورِ وَلَا بُدَّ أَنْ يَكُونَ الكُل فِيهِ قَبْلَ كُونِهِ وَلَا بُدَّ أَنْ يَكُونَ في الكُلِّ هُوَ اذَا ثَبَتَ أَنَّهُ كَانَ وَلَا شَىء معه وهو الان كَمَا كَانَ فَذاتُ الحَقِّ سُبحانَهُ وَتَعَالَى باعتبار اندراج الكل فيها هِيَ أَمُّ الْكِتَابِ وَعِلْمُهُ هُوَ الكتاب المبين باعتبار تفصيل ما اندرج في الذاتِ التَّى قُلْنَا فِيهَا إِنَّه أم الكِتَاب وَظُهُورُ مَا كَمَن فِيهَا فَعِلْمُهُ بِذَاتِهِ مُسْتَلزَمٌ لِعلمِهِ بِجَمِيعِ الأَشْيَاءِ إِذَا جَمِيعُ الأَشْيَاءِ كَانَتْ مندرجةً فِيهِ كَانَدِرَاجِ الشجرة في النوَاةِ فَالْعِلْمُ الَّذِي قُلْنَا فِيهِ إِنَّهُ هُوَ الكتاب المبين مرآة لِلذاتِ التى قلنا فيها أنها

بسم الله الرحمن الرحيم

الْحَمْدُ لِلَّهِ الَّذِي أَخْرَجَ مِنَ النُّورِ مَا أَدْرَجَ في القلم وأبرز إلَى
الْوُجُودِ بالجود ما أَكْنَزَ في الْعَدَمِ - وَفَتَقَ مَا رَتَقَ وَأَظْهَرَ ما كتم
- وَعَلَّمَ بِالْقَلَمِ الْمُلَقَّبِ بأم الكتب واللوح المحفوظ المسمى
بالكتب الْمُبِينِ مَالَمْ يَعْلَمْ - وَفَصَّلَ وَقَدَّرَ في النفس ما في الْعَقْلِ
أَجْمَلَ وَقَضَى وَحَكَّمَ وأخرج اللوح بِيَمِينِهِ مِن يسَارٍ كَمَا أَخْرَجَ
حَوَّاء مِنْ جَنْبِ ادَمَ عَلَيْهِ السَّلَامُ كما قال الله تعالى وَتَقَدَّسَ اللَّهُ
الَّذِي خَلَقَكُمْ مِنْ نَفْسٍ وَاحِدَةٍ وَهِيَ الْعَقْلُ وجَعَل مِنْهَا زَوْجَهَا
وَهِيَ النَّفْسُ وَبَثَ منهما رجالاً كثيرًا وَنِسَاء وَهِيَ الْعُقُولُ والنفوس
فَفَتَحَ بِالْبَاءِ الْمَوْسُومِ بِالهيولى والعنقا صورة العالم وفتق السموات
وَ الْأَرض مِنَ الرتق الملني بالعنصر الاعظم فسبحان من عَيْن
الأعيانَ بالفيض الأقدس الأقدم و كون الأكوان بالفيض المقدس
المقدم وَأَظْهَرَ الْقَدَمَ بِالحُدُوثِ وَالْحُدُوث بالقدم ونشر الرق المنشور
وَكَتَبَ الْكِتَابَ المسطور بمداد الْوُجُودِ الْمُبْرِز مَا مَكَّن في باطن
المتكلم مِنَ الْحُرُوف و الْكَلِمَاتِ التامات وَأَتَم وَاثبتهُمَا فِيهِ وَرقم
ورتبهما ونظم وَكَملهَا وَتَمَّم وفي الفاتحة ما فصل في الكِتَاب أَدْرَجَ
وَأَدغم وَمَا الْفَاتِحَةِ في الْبَسْمَلةِ وَمَا فِيهَا سَتَرَ في الباءِ وَمَا فيها
أَبْطَنَ في التُّقْطةِ وَأضم وَابْهُمْ وَصَلَّى اللهُ تعالى عَلَى الاسم الأعظم
والرد المعلم و الممد للهمم بالقول الأقوم محمد فتح بِهِ الكِتَابَ
وَخَتَمَ وَمَيَّزَ الْبَاطِلَ من الحَقِّ وَالنُّورِ مِنَ الظَّلِمِ وَ عَلَى اله واصحَابِهِ
وَسَلَّمَ أَمَّا بعد فإني أَجَيْتُ سُوَالكَ أَيُّهَا الوَلِدُ الصَّالح لما سأَلتني أَن
أثبتَ وَارْقَمَ لَكَ في هذا المختَصَر شَيْئًا مِمَّا قَدَرَ اللَّهُ لى في تحقيق
فَاتِحَةِ الْكِتَابِ الُتي هي أم الكِتَابِ بِلِسَانِ أَهلِ اللهِ وَ خاصته
وسميته بمرآة العارفين

٩٨